PRAISE FOR RECEIVING
GRACE IN THE GROVE

"Fletcher's story is filled with recognition that God will provide for and sustain each of us. This is a story of two dedicated young people with a dream. With God's guidance a book was born."
—Coach Billy "Dog" Brewer, former Ole Miss head football coach and Team of the Century member

"This book is about family, football and faith, and a lot more. Fletcher Law lets us walk with him through some pivotal moments in his life to see how God has been present in events both big and little."
—Timothy George, founding dean of Beeson Divinity School of Samford University

"This book will show you how God can use obstacles to demonstrate his power and grace. Fletcher Law's journey will tremendously enrich your life."
—Shannen Fields, actress and speaker

"Receiving Grace at the Grove is an inspirational and compelling story about faith, family, football, and friends, and how God intertwined them into his omnipotent plan for Fletcher Law and his family."
—Doug Dixon, CAA, high school athletic director and head football coach, 2005 Riverside Military Academy Football State Champion- Head Coach

"You will be encouraged through Fletcher's journey of life's ups and downs. This story will uniquely show why the word— Amazing— belongs in front of Grace."
--Jimmy Fields- High School Head Football Coach & Ole Miss Football Alumni

"I am Don Cheek, a minor character in the Fletcher Law story. How the power and the love of God is woven into his book and life are a blessing to me."
--Don Cheek, PhD, retired professor and department chair, University of Mississippi

Receiving

GRACE

in the

GROVE

A Story of Faith, Family,
Financial Worries ... and
Some Football at Ole Miss

Fletcher Law, DMin

CROSSBOOKS
PUBLISHING

CrossBooks™
A Division of LifeWay
1663 Liberty Drive
Bloomington, IN 47403
www.crossbooks.com
Phone: 1-866-879-0502

First published by CrossBooks 7/5/2013

ISBN: 978-1-4627-2921-0 (sc)
ISBN: 978-1-4627-2923-4 (hc)
ISBN: 978-1-4627-2922-7 (e)

Library of Congress Control Number: 2013911321

Printed in the United States of America.

This book is printed on acid-free paper.

Scripture quotations taken from the New American Standard Bible®, Copyright
© 1960, 1962, 1963, 1968, 1971, 1972, 1973, 1975, 1977, 1995 by The
Lockman Foundation. Used by permission." (www.Lockman.org)

Set on the Ole Miss campus, this is a story about an older returning student now with a family overcoming faith, family, academic, and financial worries ... and some football.

TABLE OF CONTENTS

DEDICATION

The Lord heard me in my arrogance, distress, and inability. He answered my prayers when I did not even know what to pray for or even recognize the answers. He gave me great parents in George and Susan Law, my helpmate Kay, and my son Graham. The Lord gave me inspiration and mentors like Dr. Don Cheek, Billy "Dog" Brewer, Dr. Ellis Tucker, and, of course, Miss Armelia Dukes.

Soli Deo Gloria!

"In my distress I called upon the LORD, And cried to my God for help; He heard my voice out of His temple, And my cry for help before Him came into His ears"

—Psalm 18:6 NASB

ACKNOWLEDGMENTS

The Lord gave us this story.
Great friends helped us turn it into a book.

Proofreader and educator: Jean Burroughs
Tech support: Anita Little
Graphic Artist: Hal Delong

INTRODUCTION

This story was given to me, for which I am grateful. I was not looking for it. It was a time of transition in our lives. We thought things were predictable, prosperous, and on track. As we have matured in marriage, we have learned that nothing stands still. There is no comfort in knowing this. There is a comfort and a blessing in knowing that there is a God who cares for us. Our story is no different from others'. Transition is hard because we do not know the future, and the unknown is frightening. My job and lifetime vocation was lost. We were facing financial insecurity. Our family was changing and soon to be uprooted. My sense of accomplishment and prestige was lost. My past failures and transgressions would be visible to all. I was to learn that my values were misplaced anyway.

"The mind of man prepares his ways,
But the LORD directs his steps."

—Proverbs 16:9 NASB

Chapter 1

A WORLD CONTAINED IN AN OXFORD, MISSISSIPPI, FOOTBALL WEEKEND

"The mind of man plans his way, but the LORD directs his steps."

—Proverbs 16:9 NASB

My thoughts were deep as we drove from Georgia to Mississippi on Thursday evening, October 1, 1987. My worlds were colliding around me. That day was the official turnover of our family-owned business. Law-Lincoln Mercury, also known as Law Motor Company, had changed hands. My father and owner George Law had closed the deal with Greene Ford. Our dealership would open for business the very next day as Lanier Lincoln Mercury.

My head was spinning and my heart was aching, so I tried to recall the good times at "The Grove." The Grove was the grassy center of the University of Mississippi, or "Ole Miss." It was the place to tailgate during football season. On game day in The Grove, women and men dressed for competition with each other, and the great spread of food and beverages was also designed to top their neighbor's party tent. Football was king, and you had to experience the whole package—friends, good times, and Alpha Tau Omega fraternity brothers.

My wife Kay and I were looking forward to watching the Ole Miss Rebels host the game against the University of Georgia Bulldogs. As we journeyed through Alabama and on to Mississippi, I tried not to think about my last day of ever working in my father's business.

Before we left Gainesville, Georgia, and headed to Oxford, Mississippi, something else was ending. The evening of that same day marked the end of the season for the youth football team I coached. We had only ten players show up, while none of my assistants put in an appearance due to conflicts with their schedules. Although the standard number of players in a game was eleven, the referee said we could legally play with ten. I coached that last game by myself. Our team, the Falcons, lost by one touchdown. The other team, the Dolphins, celebrated like young girls at a Justin Bieber concert. That team had never beaten us in four years. This was the first time we hadn't had an undefeated season. We had poor participation, poor performance, and great embarrassment in this, the last game of the season. As is typical of sixth and seventh grade boys, the Dolphin let us know about it. There's nothing like being taunted by twelve-year-olds. We had to wear fake smiles while shaking hands and congratulating them.

For almost four years, the Gainesville Falcons were criticized for dominating the league, similar to the Oakland Raiders of old. The boys thought our coaching staff had invented the game of football. As we left for Oxford, Mississippi, I felt that everyone at the game now probably thought I was unaware that a football had two points. This compounded the collision of my worlds as we made the seven-hour drive.

My wife and I had another reason for the trip. We did not tell our friends and family why we were really going to Ole Miss that fall weekend. I was also going to see Dr. Don Cheek, my old professor and the head of the Physical Education Department, to see if I could reenter school the next fall at the age of twenty-nine. I kept the fact that I had not graduated a secret, even though I had been in college for five years. I transferred from Gainesville Junior College to Ole Miss in 1979. After three years at Ole Miss, I left without a diploma. My parents had provided funds for me to go. At that time, I kidded that the way my life was goin was no secret. I was going to be a football coach or a car salesman. When I started at Ole Miss, I was a football walk-on. The coach dropped me because of a preexisting medical condition, so I joined a fraternity and did poorly in school. Since I did not graduate, I assumed I would sell cars in the family business, inherit it someday, and live well on Lake Lanier. My wife would be able to quit her job of teaching first grade and live her life as the wife of a successful businessman. But now that was not going to happen. The business was sold. I was out of a job at the age of twenty-eight, long before I ever got a chance to run the business.

Dr. Cheek and I had talked several times on the phone. I asked

Dr. Cheek if he remembered me. To my surprise, he did. I told him I did not graduate. I remember him replying, "Oh really." I thought his voice had an unusual timbre in it. He was not mocking me, but letting me know he was on top of his teaching profession and department. We decided to meet after lunch on Friday. My pitiful grades would be laid out again for inspection. I could no longer keep my secret about not graduating. It was going to be hard to review my lack of discipline in front of my respected professor. Yes, I had earned a horrible grade point average in physical education and had not graduated. I felt I was going to display my ignorance to the world. All of this was going through my head as we headed toward Birmingham.

As I contemplated my situation while driving and listening to a George Strait cassette, my wife sweetly interrupted.

"I know you are excited about seeing your friends and all this weekend, but I think I need to tell you something. I'm pretty sure I'm pregnant. I have not been to the doctor yet, but think I am about to go into my second month—"

I could feel my face exploding in crimson red shock. I was speechless. My thoughts were scattered like marbles. I was totally embarrassed by my reaction. I had always wanted to be a dad. But this was not how I planned it.

We kept heading toward Irondale, Alabama, and The Golden Rule Barbecue. I was in a new 1988 Cougar, V-8, black with red pinstripes and interior. I wore an Izod gator shirt, pressed jeans, new cowboy boots, and was headed out to eat with my pretty wife. I looked like I had it all. Even I would have thought that a year earlier. But now I knew one thing: I knew nothing.

All I could do was keep moving, feeling stunned and numb about the changes in my life and my responsibilities.

I had been a P.E. major in the past. I was not a literature major like many of the people on the square in Oxford. But as I recall, from some previous literature class about some southern writers, the past always seems to keep reappearing in the present.

Chapter 2

A DAY OF RECKONING
WITH DOCTOR CHEEK

"And inasmuch as it is appointed for men to die once and after this comes the judgment."

—Hebrews 9:27 NASB

Late Friday morning was a day of reckoning in the beautiful college town of Oxford. We left our motel and had a country breakfast at Smitty's on the town square. I was thrilled to be returning to campus. But I had great trepidation about my appointment with Dr. Cheek that morning. I picked at my oversized Smitty's cheese omelet and wonderful biscuits and gravy. I knew things hidden would now be back in play.

We drove through campus as the students were going to their one o'clock classes. We drove past some of the widely heralded sorority girls walking to the education building, or girls going to class anyway after an Oxford Thursday night. We turned left in front of the University Circle and Confederate statue and made a left on Confederate Avenue. After the lunch hour, we went to Turner Center, which is the physical education facility on campus. The receptionist greeted us and brought Dr. Cheek to the lobby. He warmly welcomed us and introduced himself to Kay.

When considering my return to campus, I chose Dr. Cheek to be my contact. He was a very professional teacher. I felt he would give me a fair hearing about my return to school. Many college instructors seem to get very jaded after having to deal with unmotivated students like me. Dr. Cheek was a strong teacher who always seemed to be positive toward students. I thought he would address my situation fairly and do it with a touch of grace. Still, I knew it was going to be painful.

Dr. Cheek took us to his office. He was now the chair of the Physical Education Department. He threw me a curve ball when he asked Kay to come back to the office with us. He looked at me and said, "Y'all are in this together." That was a chilly and ominous moment. The "two of us" was now really three. But what were we getting into?

Dr. Cheek was always well-dressed. He was a big strapping man from North Louisiana, 6' 4", and could really drive a golf ball. After all the pleasantries, he got down to business.

With Kay's support I answered his request to tell him what we wanted to accomplish with a return to school. With all the course hours I'd completed, I was a senior. Yet my grade point average was not high enough to enter student teaching. My goals were to graduate with a teaching certificate and go on to be a head high school football coach while supporting a family. It would be more practical to return to Oxford and to accomplish my goals at Ole Miss, even as a twenty-nine-year-old senior who planned to move my family from Georgia to Mississippi.

With my wife at my side, Dr. Cheek gave me the facts about my academic standing, my academic record, grade point average, and what I would have to do to meet my goals. It was not as much of an "ouch" situation as it was a realization of the truth and a cause of deep embarrassment for me. Dr. Cheek said I was still academically eligible to continue as a student at the university. I actually had passing grades my last semester in the spring of 1982. My G.P.A. was a 1.99 in Health and Physical Education on a four-point scale. In other words, after five years of college, I was a D student with a lot of hours and nothing to show for it. Dr. Cheek studied my transcript and noted the many Fs I had earned. I had a grade of D in tough courses like Anatomy, Kinesiology, and Exercise Physiology. I also had an F in a tennis class due to cutting too many classes. The "good" grades were mostly Cs and very few Bs. He said I would have to retake many courses to replace the unacceptable grades in order to graduate. After investing much time, effort, and money in my previous education and in hopes of a future degree, there still was no guarantee that I could pull up my grade point average to a 2.7 to qualify for student teaching and certification. The old minimum grade point average to student teach was 2.3. The standards had been raised since I left school. Also, I had to pass algebra.

Then to top it all off, Dr. Cheek shared the opinion of the department's faculty with me, which hit my gut like an anvil.

8

Dr. Cheek bluntly said, "I surveyed the department faculty who were here when you were in school."

He paused. "The consensus was that they did not believe you would be capable of doing the work required if you were given a chance."

Then he told me that I could be readmitted and the choice was mine. Dr. Cheek seemed to have sympathy for me in that time of dark realization and humiliation for my past failures in front of my wife. I felt he was supportive, as much as he realistically could be. I think he told us to think and pray about the decision.

I was fuzzy-headed leaving his office. Oddly enough, only the words of the Jerry Reed song "East Bound and Down" from the movie Smokey and the Bandit seemed to sum up my situation.

"We've got a long way to go and a short time to get there."

Chapter 3

REALITY SETS IN

"Thus I considered all my activities which my hands had done and the labor which I had exerted, and behold all was vanity and striving after wind and there was no profit under the sun."

—Ecclesiastes 2:11 NASB

Our weekend football trip was much more than a getaway. Things unknown were now known. Knowledge I learned that weekend haunted me on Monday as we returned back home in Georgia. I knew I was unemployed. I knew I was in terrible academic shape. I knew I was taking a severe risk with our finances in returning to school. I knew I needed to know how to pay for school and the needs of my family next year. Most importantly, I learned I would soon be a father.

We enjoyed beautiful weather during our Oxford weekend. Georgia won the game 31–7. I know I visited with many friends, but quite honestly, I remembered nothing more than the discovery that I would be a father and the candidness of

Dr. Cheek. I spent the rest of the fall trying to learn golf with my father, George. We attended the Georgia football games and Gainesville High School games that season. Kay was set to finish her school teaching year. She was the young, cute first-grade teacher who everyone seemed to remember even as we meet her former students when in town. She taught at Jones Elementary, the small Chicopee Mill village school at the edge of Gainesville, known by most as just Chicopee.

In preparation for the baby, Kay walked, exercised, took vitamins, ate healthy, and added to our growing library on prenatal care. The year passed quickly. After Christmas we took a trip to the Liberty Bowl to watch Georgia play Arkansas. Memphis is about seventy miles north of Oxford, so we took a day-trip to drive down to Oxford and collect real estate booklets to find a place to live.

We were able to go because of a good friend's offer. Kelley McGuire, a fraternity brother who now lived in Memphis, called me one afternoon. He was involved with the Liberty Bowl as a businessman. He said if I sold thirty-five tickets he would compensate us with tickets and free rooms at his family's Holiday Inn on Elvis Presley Boulevard. I really hustled and sold the tickets. We went to the game with my childhood friend Doug "Porky" Parks and his wife Chris.

Kay and Chris sat in the back of the Mercury Sable station wagon I bought right before my father sold our business. As we drove through the mountains from Nashville, they talked as they read baby name books and baby health books and magazines. Kay had taken her ever-growing prenatal library on the trip.

The trip was a great diversion from all the unknowns. The trip became more exciting as Kay felt the baby kick while she was playing Trivial Pursuit in the car. From that point we drove into Memphis happy and excited.

We were driving through the foothills of the North Georgia mountains where there were some cultural differences, even in the South. As we stood in line at the famous barbecue rib restaurant The Rendezvous, we were in the middle of a Memphis heresy. Some big-shot Georgia alumni were in line. A report passed through the group that shocked all the well-dressed Georgians. The Rendezvours' famous ribs were the grilled dry-rub style. This did not compute with Georgians who grew up with ribs on the pit covered in tomato-based sauce. The fur coats and pearls and suits quickly departed. Barbeque, like religion or politics, can divide people. It is either dry rub or ribs with sauce. You go with one or the other. It's Baptist or Church of Christ. It's Republican or Democrat. Most folks cannot cross over from their tradition.

The Rendezvous did not suffer from the loss of the barbecue-snob Georgians. We stayed in line, which did not budge. Finally, we settled for another barbecue favorite, The Public Eye. Porky and I had no such aversion to the dry-rub barbecue and really stacked some bones.

The next day was game day, where Georgia would play Arkansas under the lights in the Liberty Bowl. Our gang hit Graceland, the Memphis home of the late Elvis Presley. It was a fun day. After seeing the cars in the King's lineup that included a couple of Stutz Blackhawks, classic T-Birds, BMWs, and the famous pink

Cadillac, we went inside his house. We went up to the "Jungle Room" and headed downstairs. In the basement, in the Billiard Room, we laughed at all the fabric sewn on the walls and ceiling. We laughed as a group at the tackiness of the room. Behind us, one member of a couple said, "This is just how I want our den." We tried to muffle our amusement. Then we walked into the Television Room, which was adjacent to the "Billiard Room." My snobbery soon turned to envy as I viewed one of the original man caves. The "Big E" had copied President LBJ back in the day and had three television sets installed to better view pro football. "He who casts the first stone…" I thought.

After a trip to K-Mart to become more winterized for the night's game, we bundled up and headed to the Liberty Bowl. Both teams ran the ball a lot. John Kasay, Jr., a freshman reserve, was called on to kick a winning thirty-nine-yard field goal to give Georgia the win as time expired.

After the game, I ran into John Kasay, Sr., a Georgia guard from the 1966 Cotton Bowl team and former Georgia coach. I had known him as a coach when I went to the University of Georgia football camp when I was in elementary school and junior high school. He was known as "Mother Kasay," because he used to discipline guys like me for acting crazy in the dorms. "Mother" had a push-up prescription to get the young campers to decide they were sleepy enough to finally go to bed. I congratulated Coach Kasay on his son's winning kick. I also told him the good news that we were expecting a child. Coach Kasay said that one day he hoped our son would have an experience like the one he just had. I never said we were having a son, but Mother Kasey knew best.

That trip to Memphis was a great experience before we underwent a lot of serious preparations for life.

━━━━━━━━

From December through January, I worked as a salesman for about a month at another car dealership. I was number one on the sales board. Most of my customers could not get financed. The sales manager had worked with us at Law Motor Company. He was fired at month's end, and my fate followed his. This was yet another self-esteem modifier for me. This cemented my certainty that I did not want to sell cars. One Saturday I remember peeking at the Gator Bowl on the TV in the dealership's lobby. Louisiana State University was playing South Carolina. I remember thinking I would much more rather be coaching football than standing out in a cold car lot in winter, as few if any prospective customers drove up on a overcast, shivering Saturday.

It was back to trying to play golf and looking for a job until we went to Oxford. Earlier, we had planned to move in January. When we found out about the new arrival, we decided on a summer move instead. I was hired as a traveling office equipment salesman in the new year. I sold copiers, and the latest new gadget, fax machines, without really knowing how to use either of them. I did get salesman of the month, because I lead everyone else in sales, my last month there. This small victory in sales helped me feel a little more competent. Another memorable time was a trip to Oxford during Kay's spring break. She and I made the trip with my parents, George and Susan, in their big Lincoln Town Car.

There is something special about Oxford. This second trip there really changed things, once again. They changed in an almost supernatural direction. Some use the corny saying, "It must have been a God thing." I can't think of a better way to describe that trip and those few days in Oxford.

Chapter 4

HE KNOWS THE PLANS

"'For I know the plans that I have for you,' declares the LORD, 'plans for welfare and not for calamity to give you a future and a hope.'"

—Jeremiah 29:11 NASB

Our spring voyage started out somewhat predictable, but its predictability soon stopped.

In April of 1988, my parents drove Kay and me out to Oxford to help us find a place to live, scout the town, and figure out how child care would work. We took off in the afternoon, planning to stop at a motel in Alabama along the way. My dad, George, rode shotgun, fiddling with his trademark pipe. He would not light up with an expectant mother in the car, but he sure wanted to smoke that pipe. Kay and Momma talked in the backseat. We had barely passed the Alabama state line, about an hour and forty minutes in to our seven hour drive, and Daddy wanted to stop—*soon*! My father could ramble on in polite conversation, but his intentions were always very clear. He was hungry, saw a steakhouse road sign, and the Braves were on television. Case closed. I had trouble with algebra but knew what that added up to with my father. We stopped at a new Jamestown Inn in Anniston, Alabama.

We unloaded the car, went into our rooms, and made plans for supper. It was still daylight. As we turned on the Atlanta Braves game, we heard a vigorous knock on the door. Next we heard an equally robust voice bellow out, "Is that George Law in there?"

We all looked at each other, asking how anyone would know George Law was in a room in Anniston, Alabama. The door was cracked, and a big bald head entered the room. It was a big bald head known by every Georgian who knew a football was oval and by many others across the South and the country. It was Erskine "Erk" Russell, the head football coach of the two-time Football National Champion Division I-AA Georgia Southern University Eagles. It was "The Erk" who was the former long-time defensive coordinator for Vince Dooley and the Georgia Bulldogs. He was the coach of the Junkyard Dawgs' defense during many championship years. This was the coach known for head-butting his defensive linemen until his forehead was bleeding, while "form tackling" them before games. He was also known as "Mr. Clean" with that always famous shaved dome (way before Michael Jordan made that look famous.).

If you were an actor, it would have been as if De Niro had walked into the room. If you were an artist, it would have been as if Picasso who had walked into the room. "The Erk" ran a signature split 60 defense that nobody else used and the double wing "Ham-bone" offense, that no one else used either. As a Georgian you knew, without a doubt, if Erk Russell walked into the room. Even though other coaches tried to be like him, there was only one guy like Erk Russell, and that was Erk. He was like nobody else.

I get short of breath thinking about his appearance in that hotel room today. At the time I wondered, was this some omen about my future?

In a strong, peppy voice, Erk said, "George, I knew it was you when I heard you talking as I walked by your motel room." Voice recognition was the only way my Dad was recognized through the motel walls. My father had a unique voice. My dad had not seen Erk, who had moved to Statesboro and Georgia Southern, in years. We were still stunned.

It made sense, though it was still inconceivable for most people. My father had not seen Erk Russell since the spring of 1981 at a party for car dealers who supported the Georgia Bulldog football program with demo (demonstration) cars for the coaches to use. This was right before Erk left to go to Georgia Southern to start their football program. But this meeting was seven years after that party.

Finally, Erk asked me what I was doing. I had known him as a kid when I attended the University of Georgia football camp every summer. I said I was going to reenroll at Ole Miss and then coach football. Then I quickly added I wanted to be a graduate assistant at Georgia Southern when I graduated. I asked him who I should call there. He growled while pointing his thumb at himself and said, "You call me!" He then said good night to all and left.

My father was known by many for his distinctive voice, which was a loud baritone in the church choir. For example, when he sat in the congregation in church, people knew where he sat just by his booming voice in worship And yes, this added to family lore about him. Incredible things like this kind of voice recognition in faraway places like motels on family vacations have happened to him before. But this had never happened with celebrity football coaches, though it has happened at other motels with friends while he was on vacation. He was known as "Junebug" by his old high school football teammates and later by his grandchildren. Often we just say, "It was just another Mr. Magoo or Junebug moment" when things like that happened with Daddy.

As usual, my father was excited about this, and then went back to normal. Later, we went to eat supper at a chain steakhouse and returned to our room to watch the Braves. We departed for Oxford the next morning, still feeling a sense of amazement. This trip had started with a positive jolt. We did not know then that everything would be as unplanned and that we would be so unprepared yet blessed by the events.

Chapter 5

BLESSINGS IN THE CITY

"Blessed shall you be in the city, and blessed shall you be in the country."

—Deuteronomy 28:3 NASB

We arrived in Oxford the next day in mid-April. We made plenty of stops for the expectant mother and to make sure my father had time for snacks and break time to smoke his pipe. We checked into the Oxford Holiday Inn and prepared for our task.

First, we again checked in with Dr. Cheek at the physical education office. He had prepared a clear outline of courses I needed to take when I returned to school. After our meeting with Dr. Cheek, we made sure Momma and Daddy had a good supper. We left my parents at the Holiday Inn to watch *Jeopardy* and *Wheel of Fortune*. Kay and I then set out to find an apartment. We did not go to a real estate office. We set foot on University Avenue to dream about the perfect place near school and town. University Avenue connected the university to downtown Oxford. It was mostly residential apartments and homes, along with a few churches. We did not look for an apartment in a conventional way; we did not get conventional results.

We got a big, unexpected double blessing.

In preparing for our apartment search, I thought about all the hot apartment complexes around town. I also knew those complexes were the opposite of what I wanted now compared to my first college go-round. We needed affordability, safety, and peace and quiet. We were always considering that we were going to have a child.

We parked on the square and boldly started walking where we wanted to live.

In Oxford, University Avenue intersects with South Lamar Boulevard, which connects the square with the campus. When you walk toward campus along University Avenue, it is a trip of around a mile to the front gates of the campus which is laid out in the shape of a church key.

At that time, there were many old and grand homes on this street and just a few apartment complexes. We walked down University Drive and jokingly said, wouldn't it be nice if some family had a great basement apartment we could rent? As we walked, we noticed two small cedar-sided duplexes. There were four duplex flats. I had never noticed this place in the hundreds of times I had driven up and down this street in my previous attempt at school while going downtown for nightlife or late-night eating. We prayed together for the Lord to direct our steps. It looked interesting.

Our interest was piqued as we watched an old Datsun pickup truck pull into the small parking lot of the duplex where we stood. The truck had a Weed Eater, a push lawnmower, and a toolbox in back. It was the typical handyman/yardman's truck. A medium-height man, who I assumed was the handyman, popped out. He was bald on top with hair on the sides of his head and wore wire glasses, a beach T-shirt, and cutoff jean shorts. *Yep, that's the yardman,* I thought. I asked him who managed or owned these duplexes.

He said, "My brother-in-law does." Then he said, "Follow me; he lives here."

We then introduced ourselves to the yardman who looked quizzically at us. He said, "I think I have heard that name before. Oh, yeah, you must be," here he indicated Kay, "that teacher with the great résumé we received."

Turns out, the yardman was not actually a yardman. He just helped his brother-in-law with the outside upkeep. He introduced himself as Lance Hale. He was a local accountant and on the Oxford University school board. He went on, in great detail, about how thrilled the board was to get the résumé of an experienced first-grade teacher with such great credentials.

We had gone looking for a place to live, and now it looked as though Kay would have a job.

Lance told us to follow him around back so he could introduce us to his brother-in-law, Dr. Ellis Tucker. Dr. Tucker was the head of the University of Mississippi Law School Library. He lived in the back of one of his four duplexes and rented out the other three. Dr. Tucker was short, trim, and well-dressed, formal yet extremely polite. He said the front duplex adjoining his duplex would be open in June. He said he rented to faculty and older students, the rent was $315 a month, and that we could look at his duplex later in the evening.

We set a time and went back to the Holiday Inn to tell my parents the good news. We brought them to meet Dr. Tucker at his duplex that evening. Dr. Tucker showed us his personal duplex as the floor plan was the same as the duplex we were interested in renting. He showed us the two bedrooms, den, hallway, kitchen with a new refrigerator, and one full bathroom unit. He added that the duplex for rent was carpeted and had central air conditioning (unlike our house at the time) and ceiling fans. We would have use of a coin-operated laundry room in an apartment complex about thirty feet from our prospective front door. We would also have use of the pool at the apartment complex next door on the other side.

Our small, three-bedroom house in Gainesville was in a rental area. Houses rented for about $700 per month in our neighborhood. We could rent our house for $700 and pay $315 rent to live in a better place.

Atlanta-area real estate inflation was working in our favor. We were thrilled.

Ellis was a great host, a true Southern gentleman, and a bachelor. Later he showed us his figurine collections and antiques.

Momma was interested. Daddy fidgeted with his pipe. He was ready to watch the Braves again. Daddy started to light his pipe in the kitchen. Dr. Tucker firmly told my father not to. I stood amazed. Never in my life had I heard anyone give my father a command.

It was the ultimate study in white Southern older men. One was from a "good ole boy" football culture. The other was from the Fine Arts Department. My father put the pipe up, followed by an awkward silence. We departed after agreeing to mail in a deposit. Everyone left happy. Kay looked like a shoo-in for a teaching job. Momma knew we had secured a safe place for her grandchild to live. Daddy got back to the motel to watch the Braves again on television. And Dr. Tucker got a new renter: us.

The trip had been a tremendous success.

We later learned my academic plans were solidified as was Kay's job. But although we had discovered a great affordable place to live, we still had a huge thing we had to secure—child care. We figured we would have all summer to get that taken care of, and that is a story in itself. We marveled again at our blessings: a job, a great affordable place to live, and a great neighborhood.

But now we were returning home to Gainesville to get a baby born.

Chapter 6

LIFE CHANGES EVERYTHING

"Behold, children are a gift of the LORD, The fruit of the womb is a reward."

—Psalm 127:3 NASB

Time seemed to fly as we waited for the birth of our child. I sold office equipment until June. Kay continued to teach at Chicopee Mill Village School and took maternity leave the last few weeks of school. Our savings and the money we saved from selling cars and office equipment, Kay's job, and the rental of our house would finance us for two years.

We had a local moving company ready to move us immediately after the Fourth of July. I would attend the second session of summer school at Ole Miss. Kay would stay with the baby all day until school started after Labor Day at Oxford University School. We were set and in control of everything.

But we should have realized we couldn't control anything.

The baby's due date was May 28. That date passed, as did another day and another day and another day. Meanwhile, we were loving life, waiting for the big day.

When big events happen, even the details are magnified in our memories.

Kay and I were lying in the bed watching television way past midnight. We were talking with *Green Acres* on in the background. We were watching on channel 17, the old TBS, Turner Superstation, as it was known then. We had been laughing all night and, all of a sudden, Kay said, "My water just broke."

Kay was prepped, packed, and ready to go. We headed to Northeast Georgia Medical Center, which was a two-minute drive from our house.

I called her mother in Watkinsville, Georgia. Kay's mother and father were at the hospital by daylight. Soon my parents and my sisters Helen, Elizabeth, and Susan were there. Kay had a cheering section, but no one could see her. We waited and waited and waited. The nurses insisted she be given every opportunity to have a natural child birth.

Kay is 5'1" tall. She had been told by her doctor all her life that she would have a Cesarean section delivery during childbirth. Later, a friend even called me and asked what day our child was born. I said, "June 8." This was an easy date for a Georgian to remember.

Number 8 was the number of Buck Belue, quarterback for the

1980 National Champion Georgia Bulldogs. This would be an easy date to remember.

There was one problem: Graham was born late and on June 9. We still have the pewter cup with the wrong birth date of June 8 that a friend gave us after I gave them the wrong date. This birth went into overtime.

After midnight on June 9, the hospital said Kay would have to have a cesarean section. We could have told them that over twenty hours before their breakthrough decision.

Kay had known that for years. She knew from Momma that Law babies had a history of being big. Most of us were around nine pounds.

Oh well, ten days late we were ready to go. Kay was rolled into the operating room. Due to the new trend of wanting fathers in the room during delivery, I also was in scrubs and ready, very reluctantly, to meet Kay's needs. As we went into the delivery room I noticed that it was 1:30 a.m.

During the delivery, I developed a case of hiccups like I have never had before or since. My gut seemed to spread. I thought, "Am I having sympathy pains?" Why would I think that?

One of the doctors said, acting very disturbed, "Do we have to have him in here?"

I thought, *Bubba, that's two votes against having me in here, counting mine, but we ain't gonna win.*

I sat behind Kay's head. There was a short curtain spread over her abdomen so I could not see anything that might upset me. It all seemed like a dream sequence in a sitcom like the old television show *Bewitched*. It was as though dry-ice steam was hiding everything else in the world. Before I knew it, the doctor lifted my baby out of his mother, my lovely wife, with both his index fingers and thumbs on the side of the baby's neck, right below the baby's ears. I clicked a picture with our new camera. It flashed. He was, I saw, without a doubt, a boy. I was ecstatic and wobbly. I asked the doctors if they wanted a new-baby cigar. They sternly responded with an "I can't believe you asked me that" no. A new non-tobacco policy had just been put into effect at the hospital.

I was surprised by their reactions. I knew most of the crew in surgery through church, parties, or the car dealership. They now had an anti-tobacco religion. The conclusion of the night was stunning and strange. Kay was whisked away to the recovery room, and I did not know where it or she was. I would not see her until late the next morning. I got to break the news to all remaining visitors, who now were only the grandparents and my Aunt Sybil, who had joined them in the waiting room. I remember Daddy asking me how long the birth took. He had a thing about times.

I said it must have been forty-five minutes to an hour and a half.

Later, I looked at the birth certificate.

Time in: 1:30 a.m. Time of birth: 1:31 a.m.

They operated as quickly as a NASCAR pit crew, yet it seemed delayed and deliberate at the time.

As I described, I was not a valid or viable witness or helper. As Kay was rolled away to her recovery room, I was pointed by the nurses to the hallway leading to a window through which babies could be viewed. In this large hospital, it was surprising that my son was the only baby there at this time. We were there so long. During the time we were at the hospital, several mothers had come and gone with their babies after delivery.

Dr. Hosford, our pediatrician—or Dr. Mike as we and other parents called him—was the one who waved me back to the viewing room. It was around 2:00a.m., and the viewing room was empty.

It was me alone with the baby. I just stared at him. I laid my face on his torso above his umbilical cord. While laying my face on his skin, I realized that he was intensely warm but couldn't easily understand why. Then, it struck me: "He is not warm because of the lights he is under; he is warm because he has been baking inside his mother's womb," I thought. This revelation almost made me black out. My legs then buckled.

I was too tired to pass out now. I left the baby in the display room and walked into the hall. As I did, Dr. Mike carried my boy to me and said I got some bonus time since the maternity area was now empty. I got to hold my son. Dr. Mike said he knew I wanted the measurements that all fathers wanted. He pulled out a tape measure and said, "Manhood check."

My inclination was to laugh, but I was too emotionally and physically whipped to make a sound. After I left Dr. Mike and my son, I headed home with a box of cigars that nobody but me wanted or was even with me to smoke. I pulled into my driveway. My in-laws were staying in our extra bedroom and already asleep. I stood in my driveway and smoked a dried-out stogie from the box I bought at Purdue's news stand on the square in Gainesville. Being a novice and special-occasion-only smoker, I did not realize the smokes were now as dry as leaves. I puffed away anyway.

I felt blessed, relieved, and somehow I knew the Lord was taking care of us.

Chapter 7

WHAT'S IN A NAME?

"He who has an ear, let him hear what the Spirit says to the churches. To him who overcomes, I will give some of the hidden manna. I will also give him a white stone with a new name written on it, known only to him who receives it."

—Revelation 2:17 NASB

One day, the Lord will give all His people a new name in heaven that is known only by Him.

Our dilemma while Kay was still in the hospital was that we had to have a name here on earth for our baby before they could be checked out of the hospital. Kay was to be released after the second day after the birth. She began having severe headaches, and the doctors prescribed her a new caffeine treatment to stop the pain. This, however, made her sick to her stomach, so she needed to rest for one more day in the hospital.

The nurse came into her room to get our baby boy's name

before she and our son could be released. We told her we would have a name by the end of the day.

In the previous three days, I was in and out of the hospital, being absolutely no help. When my son was away getting circumcised, I was in Kay's hospital room eating a cheeseburger and onion rings. The smell made Kay sick. The next day, I went to my weekly lunchtime Gainesville Jaycees meeting at the L & K Cafeteria. I was asked by the Jaycees' President, J.C. Smith to make a birth announcement before the meeting and unload the rest of my stale stogies. After the announcement, the crowd chanted for the name. I gave them one: "His name is Erskine Herschel Law." The crowd went wild. Of course, I had used Coach Erk Russell's first full name and Herschel for Herschel Walker, Georgia's Heisman winner and folk hero.

After I left to drive back to the hospital, I hoped no one thought I was serious about that name.

I was getting concerned. It was the second day. My son had to have a name before he left the hospital according to hospital policy. George was a choice since that is my father's name. But that is also my brother Hammond's first name, and I figured he had dibs on that for a future son. We looked at biblical names, and Kay and I both liked Luke. My favorite all-time Georgia football player and Super Bowl VII Most Valuable Player was Jake Scott. Kay and I were heavily considering, before heading to the hospital, Jacob, Luke, or Graham.

We thought Graham was a distinguished name. We had a copy of Billy Graham's book *Peace With God* on our coffee table at home. We both admired Rev. Graham and knew he was a man of great integrity.

Kay had wanted to keep any name consideration secret. She had heard of other folks getting ideas about names from other couples and then using them first. Also, we wanted to see what our boy looked like before naming him. We both strongly felt the expected baby would be a boy, and we wanted his name to match his personality. I used to tell Kay her neck smelled like burned cinnamon as we spent the months waiting for the birth. I took that as an indicator that she had a boy baking.

People always seemed to ask if I wanted a boy or girl. I never hesitated to say a boy. I would think about Psalm 37:4, which describes delighting yourself in the Lord and how He would give you the desire of your heart. This was an occasion where people did get mad when I quoted Scripture. But that was a desire of my heart. I used to tease Kay that she got three chances for a son. After that, I said I was going to an orphanage with a stopwatch to check forty-yard dash times. Surprisingly, that did not go over well with folks.

We constantly prayed for the baby's health. On Kay's second evening in the hospital, I went to the Jaycees' cookout at the American Legion. By the shores of Lake Lanier, my friend Doug "Porky" Parks came over and asked me what was wrong. I told him we were not settled on a name.

He said, "I know you want to name him Jake."

I asked him how he knew.

He said it was obvious. He had only known me since I was two. Pork said "You were a defensive back in high school football. Jake Scott was your favorite player and in your opinion the greatest D-back who ever lived. Case closed." I went back to the hospital for the evening.

The next day was naming day. We had to fill out the forms before we could go home. Kay and I talked about the final name that would be for keeps. I was leaning towards Luke or Jake. Kay was recovering from childbirth and coming off medication. She wanted to name him Graham and threw in my name, Fletcher, as the first name to swing the deal.

She became emotional right about the time our friends Greg and Allison came to visit. Greg was one of my best friends, and his wife Allison was a first-grade teacher and a young very "old-school" Southern lady. She was always low-key and poised. In college, she was the college "May Day Queen," representing her sorority at Brenau University as the brightest of all the young Southern ladies.

We were about to be visited by great friends, and I had just caused the young mother to burst into tears right about the time they knocked on the door. She really wanted his name to be Graham. A crying young mother, friends knocking on the door, and the deal was now done; Fletcher Graham Law was his name.

Later, Kay would reassure/console me that any future grandson could be named Fletcher Graham Law, Jr. so he could be named after both me and Graham.

To say she was a protective mom is an understatement. She made me check every nurse who came into the room for an ID. She said no one was going to steal her baby. I thought she was crazy in her post-baby euphoria. The next day we were watching the news on CNN. Sure enough, one of the lead stories was "baby stolen from a North Carolina Hospital." I finally agreed to give in to the mother's wishes to check all the nurses' for ID, as her eyes shot lasers through me while we heard the news report. We finally left for home the next day with Graham. I was delighted as the Scripture said, "Delight yourself in the LORD; And He will give you the desires of your heart" (Psalm 37:4 NASB).

I prayed once, "If You give me a boy, I'll take him everywhere I go." I think this actually got a few people miffed that we had a boy. I was now getting ready to take this boy and his mother to Mississippi. I was totally delighted by how the Lord had blessed us.

Chapter 8

A BABY IN THE HOUSE

"O sing to the LORD a new song, For He has done wonderful things, His right hand and His holy arm have gained the victory for Him."

—Psalm 98:1 NASB

When we got back to our little white wooden home on Park Street, near the Brenau University campus, everything moved fast and fell in place.

Kay's mother stayed with us for a few days. On the first day it seemed as if the whole faculty of Kay's school, Jones Elementary, came by. They thought Kay had been home two days, but her headaches had kept her and Graham in the hospital a day later than the doctors had planned. Kay's mother was frantic when the whole gang came over and poured into the house. She insisted the baby be held on a pillow.

This amused me because I grew up as the middle child in a family of five. But I could tell this was a nervous time for Kay's mother. There was an energy I had never seen in that room filled with twenty plus women—giddy, thrilled, and proud of their young teacher—and one on-edge grandmother. They were thrilled with the blessing of the new baby, and, I am sure, remembering their own great first days of being new mothers. The days seemed like a blissful blur. It was great fun to show off our baby.

Kay had also said some special prayers. In her heart, she wanted an olive-skinned, brown-eyed, brown-haired son, who would look like her. All the Law children were usually blond and blue-eyed with light skin. Her prayer was answered.

Five weeks rolled by quickly. We met with Adams Moving Company and had the furniture prepared to be moved. We had rented our house for August. My mother and I would be going in the first week of July to Oxford, Mississippi. We would stay for two weeks to get the apartment set up and ready for Kay and Graham.

The time went by like a dream. I decided that constant adrenaline was the reason for the accelerated passage of five weeks. I did not know what adrenaline was until the shock I received when my mother had returned to Georgia. I would be in Oxford while Kay and Graham would still be in Gainesville.

Chapter 9

HE PREPARED A PLACE FOR US

"Do not let your heart be troubled; believe in God, believe also in Me. In My Father's house are many dwelling places; if it were not so, I would have told you; for I go to prepare a place for you. If I go and prepare a place for you, I will come again and receive you to Myself, that where I am, *there* you may be also."

—John 14:1–3 NASB

On Thursday, July 1, my mother and I set sail for Oxford to set up house at the duplex Kay and I had rented. She packed a picnic lunch for us to eat on the way. We were really going to do this move.

Momma followed my little Mercury Topaz in her Lincoln Town Car from Georgia through Alabama to Oxford. Her task was to direct the setup of furniture and get the duplex ready for Kay and Graham's arrival. She would stay with me for about two weeks.

Along the way, we stopped at a roadside park to eat the sandwiches she prepared for us. We stayed in the Oxford Holiday Inn until the moving van showed up with our furniture on Saturday, and then we moved into the duplex and continued our preparations. We took most of our meals at Smitty's on the square or the Beacon, which was on the edge of town. We also attended a couple of different churches. The cable company messed up the order so we had no TV as they could not schedule service for two more weeks. This made it nice and quiet. Fortunately, Square Books was just a block from our duplex.

It was very special to have my mother during this lonely time. Momma loved Oxford. It reminded her of her hometown. Like it, Oxford was a small town. It had about fourteen thousand people plus a university population of around twelve thousand. She loved the homes and small restaurants on the square and was taken with the old Presbyterian and Episcopal churches.

Momma really put herself out to get the duplex ready for Kay and the baby. I was blessed that, unlike so many other married couples, my mother immediately had a love for my wife. This was not my mother's usual pattern with people. She grew up in the classic antebellum town of Madison, Georgia and was known for having exacting manners and a sense of decorum. Her father died when she was young, and her mother got them through on the salary of a single school teacher. My mother was known for being tough. She was the disciplinarian for five children as my father worked long hours at a road construction company for years and then as a Lincoln-Mercury dealer. Concerning child discipline, my mother never said the often spoken words of other mothers: "Wait until your father gets home." Momma took immediate care of discipline without waiting for Daddy.

When I left Ole Miss without graduating in the spring of 1982, I met Kay at an outdoor dance at the Women's College of Brenau University in Gainesville. We dated for fourteen straight days. We talked on the phone for over three hours the first day we were apart when she went home from college.

When I say I first met Kay, I mean that I probably experienced the attraction of other feelings rather than pure love that a young man has for a woman. When my mother met Kay, I can say it was love at first sight. This stunned many in our family and friends. Momma found out Kay was from Watkinsville, just twenty-five miles from Madison.

"People just know how to act from there," Momma said, meaning her area of the state.

Also, Kay, like Momma, was a Brenau girl, which was a plus in her book.

When Kay and I met, we did not know that Momma had asked the housekeeper Ruth, a godly woman, to pray for me to find a good wife. On Wednesday, the day before the informal dance in late May, Ruth prayed. She and Momma were both greatly concerned about my lack of purpose. Earlier that month I said I would not get married until after I was past thirty, which I likened to old age.

We met on Thursday.

Prayer answered.

Kay returned the great love my mother immediately had for her. Few men are blessed like that. Kay always says Momma was so nice to her because she was trying to find somebody to hand me off to and feel good about it. There is a lot of truth in that also.

After Momma and I got the duplex squared away, we visited North Oxford Baptist Church on Sunday, even though she was a Methodist at heart. We had a close, special time then. Momma went back to Georgia and George on Thursday. This was earlier than we had planned. But my father was not one who could be left unattended for long.

During the few days that I was by myself, I felt extremely alone. I had no one with me for any interaction. At least the cable guys finally showed up, so I had the television for company the last few days before the rest of the families arrived. I was watching the evangelist James Robison's show, and they had a call-in prayer line. I called them. The woman on the line asked me my concerns.

I shared my concern for provisions for my family in this time of transition, which was looking to be insurmountable to me.

I remember several questions she asked me. She asked, "Do you have a bed for the baby?"

I said, "Yes."

She asked, "Do you have a changing table and diapers for the baby?"

I said, "Yes."

"Do you have food and toys for the baby?"

I said yes again while wondering where this woman was leading me.

She said, "It sounds like you really planned for this baby."

Then she said something that floored me.

"Don't you think your Heavenly Father has prepared a place for you?"

She then quoted Jesus Christ as He comforted His people in Matthew 6:26–33 NASB.

> Look at the birds of the air, that they do not sow, nor reap nor gather into barns, and *yet* your heavenly Father feeds them. Are you not worth much more than they? And who of you by being worried can add a *single* hour to his life? And why are you worried about clothing? Observe how the lilies of the field grow; they do not toil nor do they spin, yet I say to you that not even Solomon in all his glory clothed himself like one of these. But if God so clothes the grass of the field, which is *alive* today and tomorrow is thrown into the furnace, *will He* not much more *clothe* you? You of little faith! Do not worry then, saying, 'What will we eat?' or 'What will we drink?' or 'What will we wear for clothing?' For the Gentiles eagerly

seek all these things; for your heavenly Father knows that you need all these things. But seek first His kingdom and His righteousness, and all these things will be added to you.

I appreciated the biblical counsel, but I was doubtful. She was working for a TV ministry, and I had a concern about the validity of her message from these "different" type of Christians. I did not doubt her sincerity despite my prejudice. I was living in an anxious state. I had started a path not knowing if I could get to the end, provide for my family, and finish my education. Her message made an impression, even on a doubting heart.

Summer school was in session, and I was taking seven hours. I took two academic classes and a golf class. I tried my best to study well and use the clubs my father bought me so I could play with him in his retirement.

Kay and Graham were living with her parents in the country in Watkinsville, Georgia, until they would fly to Memphis. I would pick them up from the airport on Wednesday, July 14. I knew I would meet them at the airport—that is, until I got a very distressing phone call.

Kay and I talked the day before the Wednesday afternoon Memphis Airport pickup. It was about 5:30 p.m. Central Standard Time. We covered all the questions related to a family in a long-distance separation. Then I turned our talk to their arrival on Wednesday.

She sounded very weak and worried, not like herself. She spoke words I could not believe I was hearing. I nervously asked her, "How are things coming along?" She said, "I'm not coming."

I had never heard this tone or emphasis in her voice before. My heart sank and then started to throb. She meant it. Panic set in.

There was no doubt about it. I knew she meant it. In some garbled words, I said, "What?"

She said she did not have anyone to take care of her baby, and she was not coming.

A sequence of hysterical events then ensued. I dropped the phone. I raced around the duplex and started banging on Ellis Tucker's door. In mid-bang he opened it. Now, remember, Dr. Tucker was a quiet, soft-spoken gentleman who was the university's law school librarian. He was also shorter man than I. I am a shade under 6'2'", tall, and 235 pounds. When he appeared, I grabbed the much shorter and lighter Dr. Tucker by the collar and blurted, "She's not coming!" I think I actually lifted him off the ground.

He said in looking back now was an unbelievably calm voice given the situation, "What? Tell me the problem."

In a breathless, rapid string of sentences, I told him Kay and Graham were not coming because she did not have anyone to take care of the baby.

In a few moments he ran back inside his duplex. I thought he was fleeing from me and my manic state. By the time he returned, which seemed like only seconds, he said he had someone.

"Miss Armelia," he said. "She has taken care of my nephew and niece and most of the children in our family."

I went back to where I had dropped my cordless phone and gave it to Dr. Tucker. He would have to tell Kay; I couldn't.

During my time of chaos, Dr. Tucker calmly explained to Kay that he had made arrangements with Miss Armelia and that all would be fine. He calmly and reassuring told her, "She has taken care of all my nieces and nephews, and she really just wants to be part of a family. She said she was waiting for one more baby to take care of in her career."

His calmness sold Kay on this solution, and she then agreed to come to Oxford as planned. In my crazed, maniacal episode, I turned to the only person I knew in town, Dr. Tucker. The scariest, most horrifying episode of my life flared up and was resolved, unbelievably, in seconds.

It sounded like we had a solution to our great problem. We just did not know how great a solution we had.

> But if God so clothes the grass of the field, which
> is *alive* today and tomorrow is thrown into the
> furnace, *will He* not much more *clothe* you? You
> of little faith! Do not worry then, saying, 'What
> will we eat?' or 'What will we drink?' or 'What
> will we wear for clothing?' For the Gentiles
> eagerly seek all these things; for your heavenly

Father knows that you need all these things. But seek first His kingdom and His righteousness, and all these things will be added to you. So do not worry about tomorrow; for tomorrow will care for itself. Each day has enough trouble of its own. (Matthew 6:30–34 NASB)

Chapter 10

EVERYTHING IS GONNA WORK OUT JEST FINE

"The LORD will protect you from all evil; he will keep your soul."

—Psalm 121:7 NASB

In the heat of mid-July, I drove to the Memphis Airport, alone in my thoughts and unaware how to approach my wife and infant son. We would start out in Mississippi in the unknown. I was nervous. Our furniture and all our possessions were set up in our duplex. But it was just a prospective home the wife and mother of the duplex had never seen before. Maybe a home only in idea.

She would see it in a few hours. Meanwhile, I was living in a solitary and gloomy way on autopilot. Now I was just quietly driving up I-55 to the airport. I got there and actually met Kay and baby Graham quickly as they exited the plane.

I am always surprised when plans work out at an airport, especially compared to the mega mess of the Atlanta airport.

Kay met me with Graham, who was wrapped on her shoulder and looking distressed. I gave Kay a hug and kiss and then walked around her shoulder to baby Graham. He flipped his face away from me. I did not think he was capable yet of that movement. This set me back. He was only six weeks old, but he did not seem at ease.

The drive back to Oxford became a long and, if even possible, a quieter one. We finally arrived at the duplex. Kay quietly acknowledged that she liked what she saw. Momma had really prepared our new home well. Surprisingly and blessedly, especially compared to most relationships between wives and their mothers-in-law, Momma and Kay really seemed to understand each other. All the furniture placement was fine with Kay. She checked every room. All clean.

We were then in our duplex in total quietness on that bright and hot July day. We waited for something to happen.

After a few more minutes, we got a phone call from Dr. Tucker. The lady who would take care of Graham was at his duplex for an introductory visit. We walked around the back of our duplex to Dr. Tucker's residence.

I cannot recall if Kay had said a word since I picked them up at the airport. But as we walked to Dr. Tucker's duplex, she was mildly sobbing. As we turned the corner, there stood the caregiver for our baby. Dr. Tucker met us by his doorstep. As usual, even on a hot Mississippi day, he was in a starched button-down and pressed slacks. The African American woman at his side towered over him. She was tall, big-boned, and light-skinned, and her head was wrapped in a silk scarf. She had big glasses and a very pleasant smile.

Ellis introduced us and presented the lady as Miss Armelia. Before we could respond, she calmly but assuredly took Graham from Kay's arms.

Miss Armelia said with a beaming smile, "Looks like everything is just gonna work out jest fine." She then added, "All the babies I raised have grown up to be important people—doctors, lawyers, and a heap of other good things."

Kay smiled but continued to weep. Miss Armelia then gave her orders. "Y'all go on now and walk around town. Me and the baby need to get used to each other."

Surprisingly, this made Kay very happy. We followed Miss Armelia's orders and left on a walking tour of the Oxford shops, walking the two blocks to the town square. Armelia and window shopping at Nielson's on the square worked what seemed a miracle. Kay actually kept smiling as her great burden had been lifted from her small shoulders. Although I did not understand what had happened, these two ladies had communicated with each other. As was starting to be the case, these females had communicated with very few words spoken aloud. As what became standard, I was left out of these nonverbal exchanges. Kay would usually interpret them for me later.

The day was made. The crisis was resolved. Just as Miss Armelia had said, Kay and I felt that "Everything was going to work out jest fine."

Chapter 11

MAKING A NEW HOME

"Unless the LORD builds the house, They labor in vain who build it; Unless the LORD guards the city, The watchman keeps awake in vain."

—Psalm 127:1 NASB

Well, here we were. We were all together in Mississippi, spun out of our old life. After the mother and baby had moved in, we now had an older woman we did not really know with us.

The timing of this transfer far away from home made it seem as though we were in a time warp. The eminent sale of my father's business, the loss of my job and business future, the new baby, and the move to another state covered quite a bit of time. Now time was stuck in a new and strange place amid unknown circumstances. But we were there. It was a done deal. We were settling in on our first day.

We woke early to take care of the baby's needs and I was

getting ready to prepare for class when we heard something like thunder right next to our duplex. The thin walls shook with the rhythmic, vibrating rumble. I peered through the blinds, and I saw a big older model Pontiac Bonneville, with a black vinyl top and white body. These cars were called "land yachts" or "hoopties." I guessed, from my car-sales days, that this one was a 1972 model. Here came Miss Armelia Dukes, big "Atom Ant" glasses, big pocketbook, head wrapped, flower-print dress, and all ready to take care of the baby. Overwhelmed and tired, we welcomed her in.

We understood that Miss Armelia would start in a few weeks when Kay started to teach school. She seemed to always work on need instead of time. She always seemed to know when all three of us needed her.

She was calm and unassuming as we offered her a seat in our kitchen and proceeded to be absorbed in watching us. She watched calmly as Kay prepared our food and Graham's formula. She saw where Graham slept and where all the diapers and changing supplies were. She eased around and took it all in. She was so quiet that pretty soon we did not realize she was there.

I was once again unaware of the communication between these two women. There was not a lot of talk between them, but they seemed to know each other and what the other wanted without verbally communicating.

We had talked the day before about what we would pay her. Armelia just said, "Some folks can pay this much, and some pay what they can." We said we should need her from about 8:00 a.m. until noon when Kay started school. I could adjust my schedule to relieve Miss Armelia at noon. She gave us as a fee for her services that would barely strain our budget. We were relieved. We could afford the amount she asked for.

Soon I headed to class. Everything was fine. Like Armelia said, and we felt, "Everything is gonna work out jest fine." We sort of thought it, but later on we all knew it: we now had four people in our home. Each had a role. Mother, Father, baby, yet it was the unexpected Miss Armelia, who had no identity crisis in her role in our house unlike the two new parents. She was there for the baby and us two young parents.

> Older women likewise are to be reverent in their behavior, not malicious gossips nor enslaved to much wine, teaching what is good, so that they may encourage the young women to love their husbands, to love their children, *to be* sensible, pure, workers at home, kind, being subject to their own husbands, so that the word of God will not be dishonored. (Titus 2:3–4 NASB).

════ Chapter 12 ════

RUNNING, STUMBLING, AND GROWING

"Yet those who wait for the LORD Will gain new strength; They will mount up with wings like eagles, They will run and not get tired, They will walk and not become weary."

—Isaiah 40:31 NASB

Kay loved the six weeks in Oxford when she could spend all day with Graham before school started, which was after Labor Day. Working with Armelia was effortless. Sitting out on the patio, walks on the Oxford square, time in the pool, and naps were all centered on Graham.

Life was great.

As I finished up the summer semester, I became reacquainted with Leroy Mullins, the long-time Ole Miss football trainer. I had known him from my failed attempt as a football walk-on back in 1979.

I met Leroy again at church on a Sunday night. I reintroduced myself, knowing he had met hundreds of students since we last met. But he remembered me from a strange end to my football-playing career. He told me that he was sorry about how football went, which had been the result of the actions of the previous football-coaching regime. I told Leroy of my plans to return to school and coach football. He told me to go by and meet Coach Billy Brewer, the new Ole Miss coach who had been working there since 1984.

We had been blessed with several things. Kay had a teaching job in a jobless market. We found Miss Armelia, or she found us. I was in school with a chance to graduate. Now I got an interview to meet Billy "Dog" Brewer. He encouraged me to work for the team as a student volunteer assistant. This was awesome.

Later as a family we visited a couple of churches and were warmly received. Things were on the upswing and filled with a sense of optimism and possibility.

This let me reflect on the first time I transferred to Ole Miss and a frustrating and unsuccessful football team walk-on experience.

In 1979, I transferred from Gainesville Junior College to the University of Mississippi. I was planning on majoring in Physical Education and to be a "walk-on" for the football team.

I was accepted on probation at the University of Georgia after high school. I did not want to take remedial classes, so I did not go. My mother wanted me to go away to school after my first two years of college to gain independence from what she referred to as the "Gainesville Pack" and go my own way for a fresh and new experience.

As I became reacquainted with Leroy that Sunday night at North Oxford Baptist Church, I vividly recalled my failed attempt as a college football player. I reported to fall camp with the other walk-ons a week before school started and well past the time summer practice started for scholarship players. That was a red flag to me. I knew the situation was not favorable to play. Yet, I was planning on using the experience as a squad player to help me in my goal to become a head high-school football coach.

When I reported to the field house, I was paired with about eighteen other "walk-ons" that hot August day in 1979. They were an odd assortment of folks: fat, short, skinny. There were few if any hopeful prospects to look at for a Southeastern Conference football team.

Then the head equipment manager walked in. He said, "The line forms here," as he stood behind a doorway. Right before he started giving out equipment he asked, "Who's first?"

The line became a mob. The equipment manager asked, "Who has a dip?" One short linebacker prospect tossed him a can of Skoal. The equipment manager said, "You're first."

As I waited in line one of the managers asked, "Where is your physical?" I did not have one. In fact, the coach in charge of walk-ons to whom I had talked said the school would take care of everything. I was surprised to be told to go see Dr. Claxton the next day. Still, the next day I waited in line at the doctor's office for several hours.

"That will be $100, please", the office worker said.

I hustled back on campus after the physical to the field house to get my equipment and start my first college football practice.

There, however, I was told by a coach, "Come back tomorrow."

I finally saw the equipment manager after the other players cleared out of the field house. I was then fitted with a navy blue Bike helmet with a gray face mask. I was going to walk on as a defensive back, my high school position. I was issued a red mesh practice jersey with the number 12. I was also given a very small pair of white shoulder pads.

I was curious. I knew walk-ons would take a pounding going against the scholarship players. I did not like this, but I thought, "Hey, got to start somewhere." Still, I could not help but feel strange as I knew I would be doing a lot of hitting and getting hit as a walk-on at practice.

I finally got my full gear on. My heart was pounding, and I was soaking in all of my first college football practice as I started out the door to hit the field as practice had already started.

Never mind that I was three weeks later than most and almost a week later than all the other walk-ons. As I placed my foot outside the field house door, I almost got knocked down. It was raining, and the team was coming back inside. Practice was cancelled.

I felt numb. *Football practice cancelled due to rain?* I thought.

After the early ended practice, I asked the equipment manager for a better pair of shoulder pads.

He asked, "Why?"

I told him my shoulder popped sometimes. The next day I noticed no shoulder pads in my locker. I told Tank, one of the equipment managers, that my pads were missing and asked for another pair.

He said, "Go see Leroy."

Leroy said, "Go see Dr. Claxton."

Dr. Claxton's office said, "Come back tomorrow."

I did. I waited a couple of hours.

Dr. Claxton felt around my shoulder. He said nothing. He scribbled something illegible in red ink on a piece of paper. He told me to take this to Leroy.

When I got back to the field house, the team was outside. So was Leroy. I found him under the bleachers in the shade as the players walked to practice. He pulled me to the side. He told me in medical terms my shoulder was supinated some such way and medical lingo which was foreign to me and in short, I was not going to be allowed to play.

I was in tears. He was consoling after the news. He said my shoulder would pop out one day by age forty, and I would need surgery.

He also said I could be a trainer. I asked if I could have my doctor at home see my X rays, and then I would make a decision about playing. While I waited for my hometown doctor to look at my X rays, I was a trainer for a week, cleaning up the training room. My mother later called and said the doctor saw my X ray and said there was something wrong with everybody, and that he himself should not ski with his knees. My doctor's advice was to play if I wanted to. However, Leroy said the coaches refused to let me play. I quit being a trainer. I had two weeks of college football, and I was minus $200 for doctor bills and could not or would not be allowed to practice.

After that fall, *The Daily Mississippian*, the campus paper, had a piece on walk-ons and their treatment from the previous year. The year before I arrived, they had over one hundred walk-on candidates. The pre-Brewer coaches did not want walk-ons or to bother with them. They eliminated the "problem" my year by limiting opportunities. During the previous year, walk-ons, according to the student paper, were given K-Mart tennis shoes for the stadium's Astroturf and encouraged in many ways not to go out on it.

This was surprising. Ole Miss was way down in football success, and walk-ons were not encouraged even then. Since I couldn't play football, I was lost for a purpose to really just be in school. Fraternity life was next on the list, so I joined one, floated around for three years, returned home, and sold cars for my father.

That was my experience as a walk-on at Ole Miss in 1979. My 1988 experience there was very different.

After we met at church, Leroy gave me a break, asking me to talk to coach Brewer. My problem concerning my walk-on experience was not his doing but that of the coaching staff at that time. I always knew Leroy was a good man. He was a great head trainer who cared about people.

Leroy arranged my introduction to Coach Billy "Dog" Brewer, thereby righting something he did not orchestrate. I met Coach Brewer as he was sunning on the side of the building, wearing gym shorts with his T-shirt off and tucked in his waistband. He was sitting with his feet balanced on a handrail, hiss chair balanced on two legs. He was taking a dip of snuff as he sat there with a uniformed maintenance man. He asked me to come by his office the next day.

We later met and he asked me to tell "my story," which was something he stressed in coaching meetings was important to know about players. He said he was "Dog" Brewer because he liked dogs a lot, but not necessarily high-dollar dogs. His favorites were mutts, which he owned many of. He was a man for the underdog, no pun intended.

He listened to me. During our meeting, the recruiting coordinator knocked on the door and interrupted us. Coach Brewer told him to come back because he was busy talking to a young man.

The recruiting coordinator did not like that. Coach Brewer cared for people, not status. He resumed his talk with me. He asked me what side of the ball I wanted to be on, offense or defense? I was speechless. He told me to meet him at practice the next day. I was dumb struck. During August, I worked for the coaches from 7:00 a.m. until 7:00 p.m. daily during summer practice. Each day, I went home for lunch to see my family. Although the hours were long and exhausting, it was great working with the coaches!

It was also going to be a strain when classes started. The classes were hard and demanding. My little family's resources were few and seemed to quickly dwindle away by the end of the month. My GPA required that I enroll in more classes, so I signed up for twenty-one hours. My 1.99 grade point average had to increase to a 2.7 before I would be allowed to student teach and get my teaching certificate. The more semesters I spent in class, the more I paid and did not work at a full-time job. This ruled out football. I would be in class during practices—from eight to four except for a quick lunch break. Kay got home by two-thirty and could run home for lunch. Armelia stayed until suppertime each night.

This was a difficult time in my life, but a great time. I learned about sacrificing time for studying and watching our money. We were now going full-speed in building our family, school, and work.

But, basically, something had to give at this time. It had to be football. I did not want to tell Leroy and Coach Brewer, but I had to make a choice. So I met with Coach Brewer, and he understood my situation. He popped me on the side cheek of my jeans and wished me well.

In my twenty-one hours I chose electives I felt I could earn a good grade in and retook Exercise Physiology, Kinesiology and my old nemesis, algebra. Here was reality: I would never have a degree or football or the job I wanted if I did not achieve my main mission of graduating. I had paid a price financially; now I had to pay a price in study time and sacrifice. I had to choose the things I needed rather than what I wanted. My priorities had changed.

Chapter 13

LIVING IN BLESSINGS

"Blessed be God, Who has not turned away my prayer
Nor His loving kindness from me."

—Psalm 66:20 NASB

When school started after Labor Day, each day brought a blessing.

Baby Graham was happy and content at home with Armelia. Kay was able to spend early mornings and afternoons with him. Her first-grade class at Oxford University School was small and fun. The students loved her, and the parents were thrilled with the young mom teacher. Her class loved talking about the baby as she shared pictures and experiences with them.

Graham had Armelia's attention all morning and early afternoon. They both seemed happy about that. I returned from classes at about five o'clock. I was having success in the classroom despite taking over twenty hours of class. I was in class or at the library all day. All was well except algebra, which is a story in itself.

We had fun strolling Graham around Oxford every weekend. We were invited to several Sunday school parties and get-togethers because we visited several churches, and the parents at Kay's school invited us to other events.

Armelia was excited when we went to visit the Methodist church just a couple of blocks up the street. She excitedly asked if baby Graham was going to be baptized. I told her that we planned on that. However, I was raised in the Baptist Church, and Kay grew up in a Disciples of Christ Church. These were not baby-baptizing churches. We were not familiar with infant baptism.

Armelia was also a Baptist. She just wanted to see Graham dressed up like all of Dr. Tucker's nieces and nephews were when they had been baptized at the Methodist church. There was no doubting her devotion to Graham. It almost prompted me to get him baptized after seeing how happy it made her just to talk about it.

On the Ole Miss home-game weekends at Oxford, my old roommate from the ATO house, Wes, would bring his wife May to Oxford for the football game and to visit us.

When Ole Miss played games in Jackson, about one hundred and fifty miles away, we took Graham to visit Wes and May for the weekend. May and Kay would play with Graham as Wes and I headed to the stadium. It was a great fall.

Our son, Armelia, Kay's school, my schoolwork, all were going well. But there were, of course, a couple of things I could have taken care of better.

OUR FIRST VISIT HOME TO GEORGIA

At mid-semester, we had a long weekend break, so we went home to Georgia to visit our parents. My parents were in Gainesville while Kay's parents lived in Watkinsville. We had a great weekend of visiting family and friends and showing off our Graham. We returned to Oxford late that Tuesday.

The next morning, we met an Armelia we had never seen. The always cheerful woman came in with a cloud over her always wrapped head. We could tell she was scowling below her large glasses.

I greeted her at the door as Kay fed the baby. Both of us said good morning to her, and I knew I had stepped in something when she didn't answer us.

"Hello, Armelia!" I said again, thinking she had not heard me.

There was an awkward pause for a couple of beats. Next, a bomb was dropped by the lady who was always so proper.

"I guess they ain't got no phones over in that Georgia" she snarled.

I could tell Kay's spirits dropped as did mine. We were being scolded. It was just eleven words but they were powerful. In just eleven words she conveyed that had no use for the state of Georgia if Graham was there and she was not. It cut us to the quick that Armelia thought we had no respect or concern for her. She certainly had it in for us.

Her words also thrilled us, if one can be thrilled while being taken to the woodshed. She cared for Kay and me, but her every action and breath was for Graham. We were just learning how much she cared about him. She would not let us make that mistake again.

THANKSGIVING IN GEORGIA

In our fall of blessing, Thanksgiving soon arrived. Kay and I both had Wednesday off from school, so we wanted to leave Tuesday afternoon. I loaded Kay's Mercury Taurus station wagon and filled it with gas. Kay was to take care of last-minute details.

I glanced through the window to see that Armelia with her head wrapped, fall coat on and bag in hand was heading outside. I wanted to make sure we had a pleasant departure, so I told Kay that Armelia was getting ready to leave.

Kay told me to ask her to wait. I looked outside the blinds again, and I told Kay I did not think we would have to say good-bye to Armelia.

She asked, "Why?"

I blurted out, "She's in our car!"

Kay said, "How do you know?"

I told her it might be because I could see her in the front seat, holding her packed bag in her lap. We both were shocked and said at the same time, "She's going with us!" We still did not know Armelia as well as we thought. She was in charge of a baby. If that baby was in Georgia, then she simply went to Georgia. It took two educated people—though in my case, I was trying to be one—a while to figure out that simple logic.

As we headed through Birmingham, we were trying to get on I-20 toward Atlanta. As the station wagon hit a bump in the road, our car's shock absorbers bounced, making a sound just as a bird deposited a large load on the windshield of our car.

I said ,"That sounded like a bell," referring to the car noise.

Armelia exploded in a loud cackle. "I ain't ever hears it called a bell before," she said, referring to the bird deposit.

This tickled Kay, and they laughed for a half hour despite my red face.

We stopped at a Sizzler restaurant to eat a late supper. Armelia told us she had worked at a restaurant for years in Oxford after she finished working in the fields as a young girl. We understood her to mean that this was the first restaurant she had eaten in for years. This humbled Kay and me. What did it take for Armelia to have a happy holiday? we thought. Not her family, her food ,or her plans. For her, to have a happy Thanksgiving was to be with Graham—everything else was just a great extra.

We stopped by my parents' house on the way to Watkinsville. They were thrilled to meet Armelia. Here we also called a few friends to come and see us. Meanwhile, Kay called her parents. She wanted them to know they had another houseguest and learned that all would be well with that. We had planned to spend Thanksgiving and most of the holiday with the Fambrough side of the family and Grandmother Lucy, Grandfather Jack and Kay's sisters Nan and Patti and her little brother Jim.

When we arrived at the Fambrough home, the whole tribe, including over forty Wilsons and Wilkes were there. We were loudly and robustly greeted. Armelia was concerned because of the noise and crowd. And although she was warmly greeted, Armelia was there for business. She was wearing her stern face. This senior citizen, this black woman from small-town Mississippi, was in an unfamiliar place and surrounded by white people she did not know. Still, she remained undaunted in her task of caring for Graham—nothing was going to stop her. We quickly saw another side of Armelia—the lioness side. Still wearing her overcoat, she marched across the room of people and laid a bed pillow over Grandmother Lucy's arm and instructed her on how to hold the pillow and the baby.

She then took baby Graham from Kay and laid the baby on the pillow in the grandmother's anxious arms. Armelia, with unchallenged authority, firmly told the grandmother that the baby would be held on a pillow because there were too many folks around and he could not get bruised.

My wife is almost always unflappable. There is no one who gets her off her game or alters her bearing, except her mother. I looked at Kay who had a quizzical look on her face and wondered how this action would be taken by her mother or how it would end. The whole once loud room seemed to quiet and freeze as they looked at Armelia's stern face. They looked at Kay's mother, the grandmother and lady of the house for her reaction to Amelia's orders.

Grandmother Lucy beamed. It seemed she finally found someone else who believed in using a pillow to hold a baby. The whole room seemed to breathe a sigh of relief at this and was quickly back in high spirits. I had never experienced this baby-on-a-pillow method of holding an infant, but it was approved by these two wise women. We now knew how thrilled this maternal grandmother was with Graham's caretaker. Granddaddy Jack was similarly tickled when Armelia firmly told him she was "there to insure the baby stayed on schedule." The grandparents now knew their grandbaby, their daughter, and even their son-in-law had someone in Mississippi to take care of them.

Chapter 14

THE GRIND OF WORK
AND SCHOOL

"But beyond this, my son, be warned: the writing of many
books is endless, and excessive devotion to books is weary to
the body."

—Ecclesiastes 12:12 NASB

We had a great Christmas break in Georgia. Armelia
must have approved of our families as being responsible
enough to look after Graham because she stayed in Mississippi
with her family for the Christmas holidays. After packing
the Christmas toys Graham received from both families, we
returned unceremoniously to Oxford to begin the new year.

As we drove back to Oxford on an day in early January, we
tuned in the Gator Bowl on the radio. Georgia was playing
Michigan State in Vince Dooley's last game after twenty-five
years at Georgia. He had been the head football coach at Georgia
for as long as we could remember. I saw tears well up in Kay's

eyes as we listened to most of the game. This was an end of a football era for Georgians. I teased Kay by saying that she should get part time work at funeral homes.

She asked, "Why?"

I said she could be hired to cry at the meanest man in the world's funeral.

Quickly, we entered into the doldrums of winter. The fun and newness of the move and Oxford seemed to be in the past. Kay had to get back to work, and I knew in her heart she wanted to stay with Graham full-time. Once again, I took over twenty hours to try to spike my grade point average so I could student teach. Armelia was raring to get back to Graham who she now called "Little Baby Round Head." Because Graham was delivered by Cesarean section and his head had remained a bit round as a result. Armelia took this as a point of pride. She took everything as a point of pride if it concerned her baby.

Chapter 15

MOCK THE BABY

"Women likewise are to be reverent in their behavior, not malicious gossips nor enslaved to much wine, teaching what is good, so that they may encourage the young women to love their husbands, to love their children."

—Titus 2:3–4 NASB

During winter, we really got the full Armelia experience. She had her routine, and we enjoyed learning it. She made sure that Kay or she fed the baby. She watched *Buddy and Kay*, a kind of gospel music talk show from Tupelo, Mississippi, each morning on TV. She read the Bible when Graham napped. She held him continually when he was up. It seemed Graham was always in great spirits. Our friends Jeff and Betty surprised me by saying he never cried. We felt he must have been just a happy baby. But we soon learned he was around someone who never let him cry or gave him reason to cry.

One morning as we prepared breakfast, Armelia was holding

the baby. She had rolled up in the dusk, early as usual, in her big Pontiac. We heard Graham cry and then heard a gravelly voice imitating his screech. We thought we heard Armelia say, "Mock the baby, mock the baby." She made this sound over and over until he stopped crying.

We looked at Graham. He had an unusual look on his face as he started laughing. This was Armelia's standard way of thinking: "Why would you ever want to or let a baby cry?" She did not read baby books, she was one. Sun Tzu wrote his famous book, "The Art of War" in 400 BC. Armelia had her own book about the art of loving a baby, the philosophy of which was simple: love them and make them happy.

The first month we were there, Armelia had noticed our king-sized bed when our door was ajar. I had purchased it and an orthopedic mattress a couple of years before due to my reoccurring back problems. As she peered at our bed through her big glasses, she said in a low, inspecting tone, "Where does the baby sleep?"

Kay and I looked at each other rather sheepishly. Our bedroom was right next to the baby's room. We knew the baby books would say that babies needed their own space for sleeping. We also knew Armelia felt deeply about these sleeping arrangements one way or the other. But we did not want to disappoint her and wanted her approval. It was like facing a sentinel and having to answer a question correctly to see if we were allowed to cross a bridge.

Not knowing how she wanted us to answer, Kay hesitantly said, "He usually stays in our bed."

A smile unwrinkled on Armelia's protective face. She said, "Good you got that big ole bed." And then she walked on. We felt as though we had just passed an exam, and looking back now, I know we did.

Armelia was always the lady. She never spoke in anything but a positive, affirming tone. But she got her message across with her inflections. The worst thing you could ever do around this godly woman to hurt her feelings was not tending to the baby. One evening, Armelia stayed late to eat supper with us. Graham was about eight months old. He had his bath and was in his pajamas. I needed to go pick up something from the Jitney Jungle grocery store, which was off the square. I told Kay that Graham looked as if he wanted to go with me.

Armelia worriedly said from the couch, "He don't need to go. His poes (pores) are open after that bath. He'll catch a cold."

I looked at Kay. She said, "It's up to you."

I was amused by Armelia's remark as I took Graham out the door, chuckling at that old wives' tale. We had studied colds in Health Education. Colds were not caused by baths. Research said colds were caused by germs from other people.

Graham sneezed for the next three days. Armelia never scolded me, but I wish she had. The glare from those big glasses was harsh, especially after each baby sneeze. After that, my Health Education book, Dr. Spock, and any other baby care book again bowed to Armelia's book.

Chapter 16

DON'T KNOW MUCH 'BOUT ALGEBRA

"I will instruct you and teach you in the way which you should go; I will counsel you with My eye upon you."

—Psalm 32:8 NASB

During the grind of winter, I was taking over twenty hours at school. Twelve hours in a college semester is considered a full load. I was maxing out the number of classes I could take to get my grade point average up so I could graduate earlier. My grade point average also needed to improve so I could qualify for student teaching. In fall semester, I would have made the Chancellor's Honor Roll list, only yet again I failed algebra. Among the classes I mastered were some tough ones—Exercise Physiology, Kinesiology, Tests and Measurements, and two sociology courses and more the two previous semesters. While these were demanding courses, algebra had me mentally whipped and intimidated. Worse, it was a freshman-year requirement. I was an old senior. Not good.

I needed to pass algebra to get my degree and meet the requirements for graduation. I was nearing the end of my time and money.

As my old roommate, Wes Dean, an engineering grad, used to say, "You just don't get along with Mr. X and Mr. Y."

At the end of fall semester, I knew I was going to fail algebra. I talked to Dr. Cheek about it. I then went to an academic counselor to see if I qualified as having a learning disorder so I could receive study supports in this subject. The counselor was accommodating, but he seemed to feel I had a high math anxiety level that I needed to deal with by focusing on studying and testing techniques. He suggested I request accommodations from the Education Department and talk to see the dean of that department.

Seeing the dean was like seeing wizard in *The Wizard of Oz*: you never get an audience with him. He granted me an audience. He was a bearded, balding man in a suit who looked the part of a professor. When I met with him, I blurted out all my anxiety about past failures in school and the need to get through algebra.

I assumed he was busy and was not paying attention. He said, "Stop, slow down. I *am* going to listen to you." He probably did not understand his words had given me a revelation about myself then. But they did.

It suddenly hit me. My speech had been a big issue in my life. The dean was right when he told me to slow down. For example, I was taken out of class during elementary school to take speech class. This horrified me. I had a hurried speech that I knew my friends tolerated and often made comments about. I assumed people were not going to listen to me. This was heightened, I figured, because of being the middle child from a large family and a mediocre student growing up.

In big groups, like a family, a person can overreact by talking fast, thinking maybe someone not listening will understand, in the few seconds the group allows you to communicate. If they do not listen then you assume they think you do not have anything to say of importance. The person's speech then gets shaky due to poor confidence.

I have always talked fast and blurted out and felt very frustrated by the way I communicate. Bad speech is something people never seem to hesitate to critique. I was the only student in my elementary classes who was pulled out for speech, or so it seemed. But it's a boy's nature to dislike being singled out in a non-positive way.

Once I got pulled out of class, I quickly got over any embarrassment I might have for being singled out for help. I would go to a separate room with my speech teacher/therapist. She was the young and beautiful Mrs. Alice Ann Munday, who was right out of college. She looked like Marlo Thomas from the 1960s TV series *That Girl*, only much prettier and with the most perfect voice. I always liked a woman with a beautiful voice. I guess in review I know why now. My wife Kay has an assuring, sweet, and comforting voice. Assurance is something we all need. I really needed it in those days with Mrs. Munday.

I knew the dean was right concerning my voice and my problem with communication, but I would have to deal with it to get through my situation. He suggested I go talk to Dr. Bryant, who was the head of the Math Department.

The next afternoon, I went to see him. I knew I needed to sell the immediacy and importance of my predicament, so my preparation included gathering all my information and using my biggest gun. Yes, I took my baby in my arms and made my case for help in getting a degree and teacher's certificate. I sold why I needed help, with exhibit A: my baby who I needed to get a degree to help feed. I questioned if I should have done. But this was now or never concerning graduation.

My first impression of Dr. Bryant was that I had seen him before. He was tall and athletic and one of the few professors who played intramural football with the students when I was in a fraternity.

I noticed him playing in my first go-round at Ole Miss. Following the Dean's advice, I slowly made my case about being at the finish line of graduating and needing to provide for exhibit A, this baby.

Dr. Bryant listened and said he wished I had come to him earlier in the semester. He said to come see him at the beginning of second semester, and he would place me with a selected teacher and with a study plan. He also suggested getting a tutor and listed several. In the middle of listing names he said, "And my daughter Casey, even though she is my daughter, she is a fine tutor."

That sounded good to me. Sold.

I started the semester on the front row of the large class. That was what all the study help books said to do. When a short, young coed asked to switch places, I hated to turn her down but said no. I needed to let my teacher, who had a class of about eighty students, know I was there every day.

We had these bolted-down swivel chairs in class. There were some frat guys who drank coffee and read the newspaper in the back. They seemed to ace all the tests. Many students cut class, and they still seemed to do well. I had to hear giggles a few times for my simpleton questions concerning algebra. But I labored through the work of studying and passed the first few weekly tests. Then the academic tide started turning—the wrong way.

A couple of nights a week I would go to Casey's condo. It was in a remodeled old African American mortuary. We would slug it out studying as friends came in and out of this neo-hippie pad. Money was tight, and I often bartered components from my stereo to make payments.

Casey worked hard with me. She was known as the person who led a one-person protest against the chain bookstore at the Oxford mall. The bookstore would not sell the controversial *Satanic Verses* written by Salman Rushdie. This novel was about Mohammad and led to death threats being aimed at the author. This was an international news item.

It was things like this that made Casey almost the anti-Ole Miss girl. Academics were her priority. There was no sorority affiliation for her, and she was proud of that fact. Her dress was more Cal-Berkeley rather than the always dressed-up sorority girl style seen in Oxford. With Casey, I got to see a side of Ole Miss students I had not seen before. I think she was bemused concerning my Baptist upbringing and by hearing the old man's views of my twenty-nine-year-old self.

Toward the end of winter semester I got great news from the education office. Exams were coming, and I found out I could graduate that spring due to my projected grade point average, if I passed algebra. I could then take more classes in the summer, student teach, and receive my teaching certificate the following fall, post graduation.

I studied hard, but I knew passing was doubtful. I took the test. Having a sense of dejection, I immediately went to see Dr. Bryant after the exam. He called my instructor, a young graduate student who was under his supervision into his office and asked him to bring the exam.

As I waited outside Dr. Bryant's office I could hear some muffled yet intense conversation. I was told to study and come back in one hour. I retook the test. My instructor and Dr. Bryant monitored and graded it. Dr. Bryant wrote a big red 60 on the paper. He looked at the young instructor and declared like a judge, "A 60, that's a D. Law passes. Do you agree, graduate assistant?" My young instructor nodded. I felt like a defendant getting a not guilty verdict.

Victory!

I would graduate college.

Chapter 17

CELEBRATE!

"And bring the fattened calf, kill it, and let us eat and celebrate."

—Luke 15:23 NASB

Three great things happened for us in the spring: I graduated, we celebrated Graham's first birthday, and we finally met my hero, Archie Manning. We were blessed and celebrating without a doubt God having His hand on us.

ARCHIE

All my childhood friends know I have three football heroes: Archie Manning (Ole Miss quarterback 1968–70 and a long-time NFL quarterback), Herschel Walker (Georgia Heisman winner and running back 1980–82 and long-time NFL player), and Jake Scott (Georgia safety 1967–68, Super Bowl MVP, and long-time NFL player).

On one occasion as my family and I were leaving Smitty's

Restaurant, I saw Archie and his boys Cooper, Peyton, and Eli—all schoolboys then—along with his wife and former Miss Ole Miss, Olivia.

I was tongue-tied. My wife sensed this and called me away. She sensed a potentially awkward approach on my part and called my Archie-stalking attempt off. She knew I wanted to talk to them. I surprised myself and spared the Mannings. If the time arose again, I told myself I would meet Archie—and it did.

After knocking out schoolwork that spring, we got to enjoy some family time in Oxford. During the weekend of the spring football game, known as the Red and Blue Game, we had May and Wes over to picnic and see the game.

The Red and Blue Game featured an alumni halftime game with Ole Miss alumni playing each other. I learned that Archie Manning, the retired NFL quarterback, was going to be playing. He had retired from pro football by then, and he was the star attraction. He is probably the most famous Ole Miss alumnus in history. Writer William Faulkner never graduated, so he cannot count as a graduated alum, so I at least got something over Billy boy.

Near the end of the game, I said to Kay, "Wouldn't it be great to have a picture of Graham with Archie in battle gear?" She went home to get Graham, who was staying with Armelia. Our house was no more than a mile from Vaught-Hemingway stadium where the game was being held.

Quickly after the game, I took Graham to the locker room. I had access due to my short time as a student assistant with the football team earlier. Archie was hesitant as I approached him outside the locker room. I asked for a picture with him holding our baby. He asked who the picture was for. I said for our family. My guess was that he was concerned about someone getting a free ad he did not endorse. I then asked if he knew John Lee Taylor. His eyes popped up to look at mine. John Lee was my pastor, who arrived in Gainesville about the time we moved to Oxford. Archie said "Yes!" with startled enthusiasm.

In the small-world department, the new pastor at First Baptist in Gainesville was my opening with Archie. John Lee's resume said he was once the pastor of a Baptist church in Drew, Mississippi. Everybody from Ole Miss knows Drew as Archie's hometown. When I asked John Lee once if he knew Archie, he proudly said, "I baptized Archie!" Baptists have been taught "The Lord is no respecter of persons," as the good book says. But for a Baptist preacher in Mississippi, to baptize Archie is akin to having baptized the apostle Paul or at least Ole Miss' biggest folk hero.

After my John Lee reference, Archie opened up. A double-named Baptist preacher who baptized him as a baby leveraged Archie into letting us have the photo. I got to follow Archie into the locker room where I took the picture with him in the Rebel red uniform, with eye-black, holding my boy.

Awesome!

Only one thing ruined the photo. A sixty-plus-year-old man, who had participated in the alumni game, bending over in just his jock, was dressing behind Archie.

Oh well. That's one reason we have scissors.

GRADUATION

Graduation came in early May. Momma and Daddy drove over. The ceremony was held in Tad Smith Coliseum, also known to Ole Miss basketball fans as the TAD Pad.

We did it! I got the diploma and the pictures to prove it. I remember sitting on the floor of the "Tad Pad" in a fold-out chair. Many people skip their college graduation, but I figured too much had been invested in too many ways to miss the celebration. The year before the university had Vice President Dan Quayle speak. My year in the class of 1989 we had a speaker who said in his speech that no one remembers the graduation speaker. He was right. I do not remember who the speaker was. But graduating was a milestone we had reached.

I was a college graduate!

I had always doubted I could get a college degree. This was a nagging dread I had that I would fall short of. But the Lord provided. He had made a way—it was just an interesting path. It was a late yet great accomplishment for my family and myself. It took a lot of folks—my family, teachers, and Armelia. Letting people help me was something I had to learn.

FIRST BIRTHDAY

Graham's birthday, June 9, was on the horizon next. Graham was really only around us and Armelia and Dr. Tucker most of the time. Kay invited her first-grade class to Graham's birthday in The Grove. The kids went berserk, as expected. Good thing we had the space for it. Armelia led Graham, who was now walking, around by the hand, showing him off and making sure none of the first graders knocked down "Little Baby Round Head" were her delights. He was happy until I picked him up to leave. Then he sunk his teeth on my trapezoid like a little wolverine. He really wanted those kids to stay and party on.

It had been a great year. Looking forward, I would take some courses in the summer. That would raise my grade point average over the 2.7 required. I would then do my student teaching in the fall. The next June, we would move to wherever our jobs in education would take us. But our now was awesome.

Here came year two. We could not look past the now as the Lord was blessing us and we seemed to bathe in it.

Chapter 18

SUMMER AND YEAR TWO

"He who gathers in summer is a son who acts wisely,
But he who sleeps in harvest is a son who acts shamefully."
—Proverbs 10:5 NASB

With all the highs we were enjoying, there had to be a time when things settled down. Money was tight, and I had planned to work that summer of 1989. We received trying news that the person renting our house had moved out, and we needed rent money to make it. We decided to go home for a few days before summer school started. There, I ran into an old friend from my car-selling days back when I was in the Gainesville Jaycees. He had sold his house and needed a house to rent. House rented! The Lord, again, had provided.

Kay was enjoying being with Graham that summer. Armelia did not have to come to the duplex since Kay was out of school, but she came by often. Even Armelia needed rest. We spent our time with long walks, window shopping at the square, and swimming at the pool at the apartment building next door. Although we were low on money and planned to stay in Oxford for the Fourth of July, my old roommate invited us to his parents' home instead. Bob and Boots Dean lived in Sledge, Mississippi. Mr. Dean was a long-time farmer on the delta and a WWII Navy veteran. He gave you straight answers, and you accepted them. Mrs. Dean was a long-time teacher at a small private called North Delta. They had four boys—Wes, Bob, Lee, and Bill—and an older daughter who was grown and moved off before I knew them.

I always told Wes they were like the Selmon Brothers who played for the Oklahoma Sooners in the early 1970s. Oklahoma had Lucious, Dewey, and LeRoy Selmon as all-American defensive linemen. I always asked if they had a "God Bless You, Mrs. Dean' sign at North Delta High School football games, like they had a "God Bless You, Mrs. Selmon" sign in Norman, Oklahoma, for the Sooner games. Wes' family probably got tired of that joke.

I spent the summers taking health and driver's education courses. Doing so would give me another certified teaching field as a driver's education teacher. We also started attending the University United Methodist Church on a regular basis since we could walk there. We had also worshiped at First Baptist and North Oxford Baptist.

Graham had his first introduction to other children at those church nurseries. After one of the Sunday night services at North Oxford Baptist Church, Kay noticed Graham smelled like perfume. She reasoned one of the sweet older ladies running the nursery had held him the whole time we were in service. When we went to a morning service at the Methodist Church we saw Graham sitting in the lap of the lady who was in charge of the nursery. There were five or six other boys crawling around her. She was African American and looked to be in her forties.

She asked, "Has your son been around black women much?"

We both thought that was an odd question. We answered, "Why yes he has," and then asked, "Why?"

She said most of the white boys were skittish at first when they saw a black woman while our son, she added, "ran as fast as he could and jumped in my lap." Little Baby Round Head had grown up thinking if he saw a black woman, she was supposed to hold him and kiss him. In most every restaurant we went to in Oxford, he usually ended up in the kitchen, being held by one of the ladies who worked there.

Small towns are great.

Oxford was a sweet and special place to live. Though we were "outsiders," people took care of us. Kay was amazed at the local cleaners. They took her out-of-state checks without any references and gave no ticket stubs when she left our clothes. Kay asked them how she would claim her clothes. The man was surprised by this and said, "If you brought a blue dress, ask for your blue dress."

That was simple enough.

We had other small victories. We made it through the summer

financially. I completed over sixty hours of coursework from July 1988 through August 1989. It then became official—I would be allowed to student teach. Dr. Cole, the woman in charge of student teaching, gave me the good news that summer. Kay and I were exhausted, yet we had made it through a lot. Kay would return to her first-grade class after Labor Day. My assignment would be student teaching at New Albany Middle School. Armelia was ready to get our school routine going once again.

Chapter 19

OUR LAST FALL IN OXFORD

"You observe days and months and seasons and years."
                                                —Galatians 4:10 NASB

It was exciting to think about student teaching. I was to report to New Albany Middle School and teach with Coach Robert Merritt. I was finally really going to be a football coach and help with the middle school team.

New Albany was a neat little town. It was about a thirty minute drive between it and Oxford. Classes ended at 3:15 p.m. This was still a farming area, so football practice was scheduled as a PE class for sixth period. Coach Hall, one of the old coaches who also served as assistant principal, told me my main job was to see that every rear end (actually, he used a far more colorful expression instead) better be in every seat, and that the bus should roll out at exactly 3:15 p.m.

Simple enough.

Later, middle school football season rolled into basketball season, and I helped Coach Merritt with that also. Again, Kay loved her class, and her students' parents made sure we were invited to football tailgates and Sunday school parties again. My parents visited us the weekend Georgia came to play Ole Miss. My school finally beat Georgia as Ole Miss Rebel receiver Reid Hines dove and caught a last-minute touchdown, even as the ball came out of his hands right after the touchdown signal. My old roommate, and lifetime Ole Miss fan Wes said he started to wish Ole Miss had lost after hearing my father's postgame comments. Daddy was saying stuff like, "I'll never go to another game as long as I live. I am through with the Dawgs." It was pitiful, yet amusing to us all. He kept talking as if losing the game were a terminal disease. Wes said if he could, he would have reversed the score because Daddy sounded so despondent.

Two weeks later that fall, Rebel football player Chucky Mullins became paralyzed after a hit against Vanderbilt. This player always wore a smile and always fought the good fight for almost two years before going home. Chucky was an underdog from his roots in Alabama and a player whose attitude got him a scholarship at Ole Miss. The campus still remembers him because his bust and a plague with the words "Never Quit" are by the field entrance the team runs out onto the field from today. His life and lore are forever linked with all Ole Miss heroes.

Armelia was enjoying fall and liked things just the way they were. One day I was leaving the physical education building, otherwise known as Turner Center, and I cut through the coaches' office to the commuter parking lot. As I did, a female voice cried out, "Hey, Fletcher."

This surprised me, as no young female on campus would know who I was. It was my friend Margaret from my previous Old Miss days. She had just dropped off Max, her husband who was the new football recruiting coordinator. I told her to come meet my baby at the duplex later that day and gave her directions. Margaret did drop by, and I introduced her to Armelia. Margaret complimented baby Graham on his looks and how smart he was, but Armelia did not like having a female visitor at all, and her voice was suspicious and hesitant in conversation. "Pretty? You ain't never seen pretty until you seen Miss Kay," she responded. Or, "Smart? You ain't never seen somebody so smart as that Kay, you know she teaches school she so smart. there ain't a woman around Mississippi as smart and pretty as she, none that could hold a candle to her she…"

Margaret quickly understood what Armelia was thinking, and she politely left. We were in the presence of a lioness, and nothing and no one was going to mess with her home. And nobody or nothing was going to mess up Little Baby Round Head's home either.

Armelia loved taking Graham for walks in his stroller. We would block off the driveway and watch him spin his four-wheel walker around the parking lot. Armelia, though, was starting to act a little different, and this concerned us.

That summer Armelia's big Pontiac got rear-ended, which left her without a car, so I picked her up in the morning, and Kay took her home in the evenings. Along the way, she and Kay would drive through Danver's to get Armelia's favorite meal – a roast beef sandwich.

Armelia was getting older. She was more willing to rest now when the opportunity came, though she still had her daily routine. She liked to read my Bible because of the study notes, so we decided to give her one of her own. We took her to the Christian bookstore one day where she picked out a high-dollar, genuine leather edition. I gritted my teeth at the price, but Kay's eyes told me to buy it. Armelia deserved anything from us we could give her. We had her name engraved on it. She read it often.

Armelia did find something from Georgia she did like—my supply of canned Brunswick stew. That particular brand was not sold in Mississippi. Momma made sure I had many cans to get me through our stay. The further away from Georgia, the harder it gets to find it. In fact, Georgia Brunswick stew is very different from that in other regions. Once I ordered it from a barbecue restaurant in Alabama. It tasted like vegetable soup. My special stash of stew was just that—special. I told Kay that it was mysteriously dwindling, and Kay let me know that Armelia was more special.

Armelia still liked the *Buddy and Kay Show* from Tupelo and *The Beverly Hillbillies* on TV. When we got home each day, she would laugh and give us an update on what Granny Clampett said that day. One day she told Kay, "I don't think that Granny is near as old as she acts out to be."

She also liked Oprah and watched her with great interest "That Oprah is from Mississippi and tells some practical things," she said. Cable TV really opened up her world. Later, we found out she had a "rabbit ear" set that only got a couple of fuzzy stations. We realized we took a lot for granted.

Armelia never complained, regardless of her circumstances. One afternoon when we got home, she seemed to be in an unusual mood. She had a frown on her face. She said the TV was too loud to watch that day. I had a twenty-five-inch Curtis Mathis model, which was big stuff back when I sold cars. It had an alarm. I had the alarm on high to wake us each morning, after which I would turn it down and then off. But that morning I forgot to turn down the volume. Armelia did not know you could adjust the sound on the remote control.

We knew Armelia seemed sad toward the end of the fall. It never occurred to me she was already moping about our departure and especially Little Baby Round Head. Age was catching up with her. She told Kay her grandson was coming to visit her. Kay said she would make some cookies for him, but Armelia said, "I don't think he wants no cookies, he has the sugar diabetes."

Kay was shocked at the news of a diabetic child. She asked, "How old is your grandson?" Armelia told Kay he was forty-eight.

Kay and I both thought, how old is this woman?

One Saturday in November, Kay and I had to take the National Teacher's Exam, which was a standardized teaching test. With the right score I would get my teaching certificate in Mississippi, and Kay could get her license transferred from Georgia. The test was to be given early in the a.m. and would resume in the afternoon after a lunch break. We asked Armelia to spend the night with us because we would be up early on Saturday for this test. She was happy to stay with us and slept in Graham's room on a trundle bed. Graham started crying about 1:30 a.m. Kay rushed in to get him so as not to disturb Armelia. After Graham was quieted in our room, I heard a rumbling in his room. I ran out to the hallway. Armelia had her coat on, head wrapped, and bag in hand. She said in a disgusted, broken voice, "Youse can just take me home now, I guess since y'all don't need me no more."

Nothing could break your heart faster than seeing a distraught Armelia. Her face pointed down from her tall frame, and she would look through and over her big-rimmed glasses. Her voice had a gravelly squeal to it. Not knowing what to do, I hurriedly ran to our bedroom and told Kay that Armelia was leaving. Kay hopped up from the bed and quickly handed me the baby. Kay made up with Armelia as we got her back into bed in Graham's room with him in his baby bed.

Armelia, as far as we could see, had one joy, one duty she was here on Earth for. That joy and duty was to take care of her baby Graham. And we, the parents, were stopping her. He was her every thought. Again Armelia made us sit back in awe at her total devotion to our son.

We set out that morning to take the teacher test, and things were back to normal for Armelia. Kay finished the test well before I did. She went to the duplex and took Armelia home to rest. She then got a Yerk's sub and had it waiting for me, as she knew I would be watching college football on TV when

I arrived later that afternoon. The Lord had surely blessed me with my beautiful and thoughtful wife.

I knew my father would be unhappy as I watched Kentucky eliminate Georgia's chance to win the Southeastern Conference with an upset victory.

That fall semester I finished my student teaching and received my teacher certification in the mail. Kay also had a great fall semester at the Oxford University School. We were heading into Christmas and would soon need to look for teaching jobs as we prepared to move. Oxford was a great town, but there were not many openings there for teachers. Although the small private school Kay taught at was excellent, we knew we would have to move so we both could find a place to teach and for me to coach football.

We knew when we returned from Christmas in Georgia that we would have a long good-bye and a major transition.

Chapter 20

WANDERING AND TRUSTING

"By faith Abraham, when he was called, obeyed by going out to a place which he was to receive for an inheritance; and he went out, not knowing where he was going."

—Hebrew 11:8 NASB

When Kay and I had started our life together, we did not know where we were going. We did not know we would have a baby son. We did not know we would move to a new land. We did not know where we would live or how we would provide for our family. We did not know we would find a new home and have such a loving person as Armelia in our lives—and family.

The Lord had provided.

Now it was the beginning of 1990. Money was getting tighter. I started to work some days as a substitute teacher at the local schools. I took two graduate classes so I could later transfer into a master's program near wherever my new work location would be. Kay and I both felt things were about to quickly change.

During the winter I went to two coaches' clinics in Atlanta. I stayed with friends in the city while I pursued teaching and coaching opportunities. At both clinics I sat through lectures on coaching and then hit the job board where positions for football coaches were posted. It was sometimes hard to find any of the coaches who had posted the jobs. I found out quickly then that some of the coaches just went to football clinics so they could go to the "gentlemen's clubs" in Atlanta. But I did get a job offer from a new metro school in Atlanta. The young head coach offered me a position as a defensive back coach and PE teacher.

I drove to the school later that spring for an appointment with the principal as this coach had suggested. I was there at 8:00 a.m. sharp for our interview. At 10:00 a.m., the principal walked out of his office, put on his leather Members Only jacket, and said, "Do we have an appointment today?"

I replied, "Yes we do."

He gave me a puzzled look, and then he left the school. I waited until after lunch for his return. I left my parents' phone number with his secretary and asked her to please have him call me. Then I drove to Gainesville after the five-hour wait.

I later called the school and asked his secretary to please tell the principal I could reschedule the appointment later that day or the next if he would call me to do so. I told her I had driven from Mississippi for the meeting he scheduled. I called even after my return to Mississippi later that week and left my number again.

I received no call.

I sent out over eighty resumes to schools in Georgia. I figured Graham would need to be within driving distance of his grandparents. A private school in South Georgia called, but I felt we could not afford the salary or moving costs.

Later, a team that had just played in four state championship games called me. They liked my experience and that I was from Ole Miss. I got an interview and after it, a job offer. I was set to live with the head coach during spring practice the last two weekends of May, and I was to coach running backs and defensive ends. Kay and I had visited the team's town on her spring break. It was a classic Southern town not more than an hour from her parents' home. Eventually, I got the job offer from over forty applicants, and Kay was excited about the prospective move.

We only had one problem. The assistant coach I was going to replace did not get the head coaching job he expected. So he stayed in his present position. No job for me again.

Kay was very disappointed and asked me when we found out, "Is this how you feel when you lose a football game?" She was learning the hard way what the life of a football coach's wife was like.

Again, I was offered a strength and conditioning job along with the running backs and defensive ends coach at a metro Atlanta class-A school that had recently won a state championship. I met with the principal and head coach, and they said they wanted me. Later the coach called me. He said the superintendent was black and he was told he had to hire a "n———." I was disappointed but glad I did not have to work with that jerk. For all he knew about me, my wife could have been African American. It was time for spring practice to start at Ole Miss. I went to Coach Brewer's office and told him my situation. He generously agreed to let me work as a student assistant for the new defensive back coach, Bob Pruett. This was a great experience, as we started in March. I learned new pass coverages and drills. I finally was going to get on the sidelines of an Ole Miss football game—even if was only the spring practice Red and Blue Game.

The spring inter-squad game ended the four weeks of spring practice. It rained hard on the Friday night before, and some people in the field house said they might not play due to the wet sod turf in the stadium. I thought that was ridiculous and that a game, even a spring practice game, would never be cancelled on a sunny Saturday.

That Saturday about noon we were bused to the Ole Miss Student Union. From there the players walked through The Grove to the stadium. This was called "The Walk of Champions" and was a game-day tradition started by Coach Brewer. Although this was a mundane spring game, not an SEC battle Saturday with LSU, it was a Sugar Bowl to me.

As we got off the bus, Coach Brewer said to me, "'Georgia Boy' lead us through." I could not believe it! I led the players through The Grove with the trainers and coaches following us. It did not matter to me if there were a piddling number of fans in The Grove compared to the regular season. As I went past the fans and trees, I thought how lucky I was. But when we got to the gate, head trainer LeRoy got the call on the radio that the game was cancelled. Oh well, I thought. College football and I were never meant to be. If I needed a sign, here it was—again.

Later that spring, I got a job offer from a rural school north of Athens. I had actually known the coach from Kay's hometown church. Most of the school's teachers commuted about thirty miles from Athens. Kay and I decided to move back to our rental house in Gainesville. It was a fifty-mile commute. I reasoned that it beat buying and selling houses for the twenty-minute difference on a one-way commute. Kay had a great reputation from her previous time with the Hall County school system and got a job over the phone. Her new school was in Flowery Branch, which was near Gainesville.

As we finalized our plans, we were always considering Graham. One spring afternoon we strolled Graham around Oxford during which we walked on the city street by First Baptist Church, where they had a fenced-in playground. A lot of young kids were playing on the equipment in an after-school program. Graham rushed the fence and started making a sound we had never heard before as he tried to climb up. He was almost two years old.

He had a primal instinct to run to those kids. He clenched the fence with his feet and hands and seemed to growl. It reminded me of the novel *Call of The Wild*. We had to pry him off the fence as he protested. At the same time, we knew he had to be with other kids soon. He was changing. We were changing. Armelia was really slowing down. We knew from the start that we would be living in Oxford for only two years.

Time was just about up. But now we were very reluctant to move.

One afternoon, I returned home after substituting at the local junior high. Kay was out grocery shopping. As I unlocked the door and entered the duplex, I was met by a defiant shout of authority. "Get out of here, you do not belong here, you leave that baby alone!"

It came again. "Leave that baby alone! You don't belong in here!" I saw a large-framed lady with the big glasses stand up from the couch and get bowed up for combat. She seemed to take me for a stranger. She must have been roused from a hard sleep, I thought.

I said, "Armelia, it's me, Fletcher."

She said, "Youse get out of here now." She was starting to step toward where I stood at the door. Concerned, I just said, "I'll come back later," and closed the front door. I had startled her during her nap and awakened a lioness or a mamma bear.

I figured of the three of us only one was not safe: me!

I drove around for about twenty minutes. Kay was back at

home and all was fine when I returned. She and I were getting concerned about Armelia's age but we still did not know how old she was. But no matter her age, her joy and duty, down to her bone marrow, was to take care of Fletcher Graham Law.

Chapter 21

THE PREPARATION AND MOVE

"I went about as though it were my friend or brother; I bowed down mourning, as one who sorrows for a mother."

—Psalm 35:14

Right before we prepared for the move, Armelia had some problems with her Social Security benefits. Kay asked her to bring her the paperwork and said she would be glad to help her. As I was watching Kay look at Armelia's Social Security forms, her eyes lit up.

Kay motioned me into the kitchen and emphatically whispered with alarm, "Armelia is seventy-nine years old!" My eyes also lit up. No wonder she was getting tired.

I rented a large Ryder truck and got a fellow student and one of the football players to help us load it. It surprised all of us how much stuff we had accumulated. Kay and I had a life together and had settled down before this adventure. We had not been the typical student housing couple.

Our last week there, Dr. Tucker came by to tell us good-bye and to give Graham a birthday present. His next party would be in Georgia. We did not know it at the time, but Dr. Tucker's health was failing and fast. We also did not know this good man would not be around much longer.

Both Kay and Armelia started acting strange the last couple of days. They would not stay in a room with each other, and they each walked around with a look that was half-grimace and half-smile. As we loaded the truck, I said to Kay, "Armelia's ride is here." One of her children had come to get her.

Kay said, "Okay," and then repressed her emotions, acting as though she ignored the departure.

I had been around these two women for two years. Now, I realized once again that I had learned nothing about their relationship, despite watching them day after day. Still, I tried to prepare both of them for Armelia's separation from our family.

I wanted to get this emotionally delayed bombshell good-bye over. I waited and waited. Still, they both walked away from each other like two magnets repelling each other. They both continued with that half-smile and half-grimace look on their faces. I realized there would not or could not be a good-bye as I watched them both with amazement.

I had two emotional women who refused to show any emotion. Armelia left with her daughter in one direction and Kay went to the back of our duplex. Meanwhile, I stood there anticipating the emotional display that did not happen at this farewell.

The rental truck was loaded. Our duplex was clean and cleared out. We were packed up, loaded, and ready to go back to Georgia. I drove the large moving truck, and Kay followed in the station wagon. As we arrived in Gainesville hours later, the transmission in the station wagon gave out. It was ninety plus degrees. I stop to pick up Kay in the Ryder truck and called a wrecker.

My brother Hammond and a friend met us at our house, and we quickly unloaded the truck within an hour. Our little house was then set. The past two years seemed like a dream.

Chapter 22

YES, THERE WAS A FAREWELL

"The conclusion, when all has been heard, *is*: fear God and keep His commandments, because this *applies to* every person."

—Ecclesiastes 12:13 NASB

"This is the very thing I wrote you, so that when I came, I would not have sorrow from those who ought to make me rejoice; having confidence in you all that my joy would be *the joy* of you all."

—Corinthians 2:3 NASB

In this true tale, I saw displays of love, care, and grace I could have never dreamed. I had my beautiful wife, who would trade her life, her home, and her future for me. I had Dr. Cheek, who stood up for me when I was helpless and needed realistic encouragement and was there for me. I had Dr. Tucker, who I barely knew, looking out for my best interests. I had Coach Billy Brewer, who inspired me by giving me a taste of big-time

107

football and listened to my story and helped me achieve my goals.

Most of all, I had the Lord, who was ever present in our lives. He knew me, provided for me, and was patient with me in my sinfulness and ignorance. He loved me, as only He can do.

And now for the conclusion of our farewell with Armelia. How can you describe someone who loves your baby as much as you do? I did not know such a thing as this was possible, but an elderly African American woman loved my son as if he was truly her own. There is a well-known passage from Ecclesiastes 3:1–4 that described our emotions.

> There is an appointed time for everything. And there is a time for every event under heaven. A time to give birth and a time to die; A time to plant and a time to uproot what is planted. A time to kill and a time to heal; A time to tear down and a time to build up. A time to weep and a time to laugh; A time to mourn and a time to dance.

Ecclesiastes 3:5 NASB reads: "A time to throw stones and a time to gather stones;" and "A time to embrace and a time to shun embracing."

These women knew it was not a time to embrace. I did not. But there would be a time to embrace. We returned to Gainesville, Georgia, as I coached football and Kay taught school. Kay enrolled Graham into a good preschool program, which worked out well for all of us.

We were never able to have any more children.

Kay called Armelia often and sent her many pictures of Graham as he was growing up. Due to lack of funds because of the two years where I really had no income, we were not able to get back to Oxford to see Armelia as soon as we had hoped. It was almost three years before we could go visit her.

We left for our visit that March, knowing Armelia's condition was quickly declining. She was nearing eighty-two years old and in failing health. She had recently moved back after living with family members in Indiana and was in her house for a brief time. We knew we had to make the trip, now.

We left on a Friday afternoon after school. We ate at the Varsity in Atlanta on the way to Oxford. As we our chili dogs, we talked about our fear that Graham might not remember Armelia and how disappointed she would be if he didn't recognize or respond to her We finally arrived in Oxford in the wee hours of the morning and checked into the Holiday Inn. We still managed to rise early to go visit Armelia.

We turned on the old gravel road to get to her house that Saturday morning. Her house was built in the old "shotgun" style and was very decrepit. Her dog, Smoke, a mutt-ish beagle-type mix, ran out to greet us while politely barking. He was a legendary dog the way she had talked about him. Graham had heard his name from Armelia's letters.

Graham loved dogs. He pointed and said, "There's Smoke!" He did look like soot and smoke like she had described. We went up the wooden stairs and knocked on the door, and she told us in a strained voice to come in. She looked old and broken-down, and we saw her encouraging smile pointing toward the ground as she was unable to hold her head up.

We both were still concerned about how Graham would react to finally seeing her again. He ran into her line of vision, got on his tip toes, and kissed her right smack on the lips. She burst in to a beautiful smile, with her eyes still only on Graham. Later, after a minute of hugging, Kay spoke to Armelia.

That's when it happened.

It was as if a window had opened on each other's face and a river rushed down on both of them.

They could not talk for minutes. Although few words were said aloud, the talking was soft. They had both finally said their good-byes, three years later, mixed with their hellos. Their greeting and late farewell to each other was on their own time and in their own way.

Now was "a time to weep and a time to laugh."

Armelia then introduced us to Smoke; Graham stayed in her lap.

Armelia was not very strong of voice, but we could tell she was happy and satisfied. We looked around her house. There were at least forty picture frames all around it. In those picture frames were various photos of her extended family. There must have been children, grandkids, great-grandchildren, and possibly great-great grandchildren, along with nephews and nieces. But over every face of each photo, a photo of Graham's face was Scotch taped over each original face in each picture. This pleased me but also caused me concern. I hoped her relatives were not jealous of the attention she gave Graham.

Within that year Armelia had to move back to Gary, Indiana, to live with some of her children. One of her daughters kept us updated on Armelia's physical condition, as she was going downhill. She soon died, and the funeral was in Oxford. Unfortunately, we were not able to attend due to how late the news of her death reached us. Kay talked to one of her daughters who told her about Armelia having had some extended hospital stays. When she became unresponsive and acted as though she were giving up, the nurses would ask her about that little white boy in the picture.

They would ask, "Who is that in the picture? What is his name? Ronald, Gary, or Glenn or something?" They knew this would make Armelia feisty. Armelia, her daughter said, would straighten up in bed and shout out, "That's Fletcher Graham Law, and he is going to be a very important person."

Her family seemed to delight in her passion for Graham. It seemed to keep her going. Her daughter told Kay, "We knew she always said she was waiting for that one more baby she was supposed to care of."

That baby was ours.

She was sent to us by a decree from heaven. We all needed her. She taught us both how to be parents.

She showed us the grace of our Lord sending his son Jesus Christ.

How can somebody love a baby as much as the parents do?

This was a waiting, providential love prepared for us in our time of need.

God cares for us.

To God be the glory!

"This is the very thing I wrote you, so that when I came, I would not have sorrow from those who ought to make me rejoice; having confidence in you all that my joy would be *the joy* of you all."

—Corinthians 2:3 NASB

SCRIPTURE REFERENCES

Proverbs 16:9
"The mind of man plans his way,
But the LORD directs his steps."

Hebrews 9:27
"And inasmuch as it is appointed for men to die once and after this *comes* judgment."

Ecclesiastes 2:11
"Thus I considered all my activities which my hands had done and the labor which I had exerted, and behold all was vanity and striving after wind and there was no profit under the sun."

Jeremiah 29:11
"'For I know the plans that I have for you,' declares the LORD,

'plans for welfare and not for calamity to give you a future and a hope."

Deuteronomy 28:3
"Blessed *shall* you *be* in the city, and blessed *shall* you *be* in the country."

Psalm 127:3
"Behold, children are a gift of the LORD,
The fruit of the womb is a reward."

Psalm 98:1
"O sing to the LORD a new song,
For He has done wonderful things,
His right hand and His holy arm have gained the victory for Him."

Matthew 6:26–33
"Look at the birds of the air, that they do not sow, nor reap nor gather into barns, and *yet* your heavenly Father feeds them. Are you not worth much more than they? And who of you by being worried can add a *single* hour to his life? And why are you worried about clothing? Observe how the lilies of the field grow; they do not toil nor do they spin, yet I say to you that not even Solomon in all his glory clothed himself like one of these. But if God so clothes the grass of the field, which is *alive* today and tomorrow is thrown into the furnace, *will He* not much more *clothe* you? You of little faith! Do not worry then, saying, 'What will we eat?' or 'What will we drink?' or 'What will we wear for clothing?' For the Gentiles eagerly seek all these things; for your heavenly Father knows that you need all these things. But seek first

His kingdom and His righteousness, and all these things will be added to you."

Matthew 6:30–34
The words of Jesus. "But if God so clothes the grass of the field, which is *alive* today and tomorrow is thrown into the furnace, *will He* not much more *clothe* you? You of little faith! Do not worry then, saying, 'What will we eat?' or 'What will we drink?' or 'What will we wear for clothing?' For the Gentiles eagerly seek all these things; for your heavenly Father knows that you need all these things. But seek first His kingdom and His righteousness, and all these things will be added to you."

Psalm 121:7
"The LORD will protect you from all evil; He will keep your soul."

Psalm 127:1
"Unless the LORD builds the house, They labor in vain who build it;
Unless the LORD guards the city, The watchman keeps awake in vain."

Isaiah 40:31
"Yet those who wait for the LORD Will gain new strength;
They will mount up *with* wings like eagles, They will run and not get tired,
They will walk and not become weary."

Psalm 66:20
"Blessed be God, Who has not turned away my prayer
Nor His loving kindness from me."

Ecclesiastes 12:12

"But beyond this, my son, be warned: the writing of many books is endless,
and excessive devotion *to books* is wearying to the body."

Psalm 32:8

"I will instruct you and teach you in the way which you should go;
I will counsel you with My eye upon you."

Luke 15:23

"And bring the fattened calf, kill it, and let us eat and celebrate."

Proverbs 10:5

"He who gathers in summer is a son who acts wisely,
But he who sleeps in harvest is a son who acts shamefully."

Galatians 4:10

"You observe days and months and seasons and years."

Hebrews 11:8

"By faith Abraham, when he was called, obeyed by going out to a place which he was to receive for an inheritance; and he went out, not knowing where he was going."

Ecclesiastes 12:13

"The conclusion, when all has been heard, *is*: fear God and keep His commandments, because this *applies to* every person."

Ecclesiastes 3:1–5

"There is an appointed time for everything. And there is a time for every event under heaven—A time to give birth and a time to die; A time to plant and a time to uproot what is planted. A time to kill and a time to heal; A time to tear down and a time to build up. A time to weep and a time to laugh; A time to mourn and a time to dance. A time to throw stones and a time to gather stones; A time to embrace and a time to shun embracing."

Psalm 35:14
"I went about as though it were my friend or brother; I bowed down mourning, as one who sorrows for a mother."

Corinthians 2:3
"This is the very thing I wrote you, so that when I came, I would not have sorrow from those who ought to make me rejoice; having confidence in you all that my joy would be *the joy* of you all."

ABOUT THE AUTHOR

Dr. Fletcher Law lives in his hometown of Gainesville, Georgia. Fletcher is a minister who has worked as a pastor, preacher, evangelist, chaplain of Riverside Military Academy, sports evangelist, camp pastor, school teacher and football coach. Fletcher is married to the former Kay Fambrough of Watkinsville Ga. Their son Graham is a college student. They like high school and SEC football, the beach and pugs. Fletcher earned the following degrees- Doctor of Ministry degree from Samford University's Beeson Divinity School, MDiv Emory's Candler school of Theology, MEd from North Georgia College and State University, BS ED University of Mississippi.

CONTACT THE AUTHOR

Fletcher Law
fletcherlawandgrace@gmail.com
FletcherLawandGrace.com
fletcherlawandgrace.blogspot.com

CPSIA information can be obtained at www.ICGtesting.com
Printed in the USA
LVOW06s0611300713

345219LV00004B/5/P